Relentless Optimism I force in my life. Yet ev
devoted to finding the i.␣
have been moments when success, or even simple
happiness, have felt completely out of reach.

But here's what I've learned: *You can absolutely build the life you dream of.*

In these pages, I share my personal journey of overcoming hardship. From navigating the end of a marriage marked by emotional abuse to building and ultimately selling a business with a partner whose narcissistic behavior pushed me to the brink, my story is one of resilience, rediscovery and triumph.

More importantly, I'll show you the path I took to move from merely surviving to truly thriving.

But this book isn't just about my story ... it's about yours too. Inside, you'll find meaningful insights and practical tools to help you take an honest look at where you are, imagine where you want to be and map out a clear, actionable path forward – whether that means improving your current circumstances or starting fresh.

Together, we'll explore how to turn hardship into happiness, transforming life's struggles into steppingstones toward the future you deserve.

After all, living the life you've always imagined is absolutely possible. All it takes is the courage to begin and the work to get there.

-RЧH

Rya Hazelwood | 1

Advance Praise for *Relentless Optimism & Other Life Goals*

"Broken relationships produce broken people, and in *Relentless Optimism & Other Life Goals*, author Rya Hazelwood shows the reader a way back not just to normalcy, but to a capacity to thrive. Through the lens of Rya's intensely personal stories, we see and feel the enormous toll that bad relationships take on our soul and our ability to cope. If you have survived a failed marriage or even if you feel trapped in one, there is hope for you. That is the central message of this book. And not just hope, but practical solutions to real-life problems like magical thinking. I appreciate this book so much because I lived through a similar version of it. Only in my case, I did not have the knowledge that Rya shares here. Now that I've read her book, I wish I knew of her strategies 15 years ago. It would have saved me a lot of heartache. Trust me. You need the truths of Rya's book. It can help, heal and encourage your wounded heart."

– Ron Starner
EVP, Conway Data Inc.
Author of *The 10 Standards of Successful Leaders: How to find your purpose and fulfill your dreams through meaningful work*

"As a psychiatrist, I emphasize resilience and mindset as foundational elements in the journey toward healing. Rya Hazelwood's *Relentless Optimism & Other Life Goals* provides accessible, actionable steps that readers can weave into their daily lives. Her approach to reframing challenges, setting boundaries and building emotional strength complements the therapeutic work of overcoming self-doubt and achieving lasting, positive change. The authenticity of her storytelling makes these concepts even more relatable and inspiring. This book is an invaluable companion for anyone rebuilding after trauma or adversity or even just working on self-improvement and dream building."

– Leigh F. Blalock, MD
Board-Certified Psychiatrist
& Mental Health Advocate

"I consider myself a natural optimist, and I've always tried to see the silver lining, even through some of life's hardest moments. But even the most hopeful among us can sometimes feel lost or in need of a touchpoint. *Relentless Optimism & Other Life Goals* was exactly that for me – a powerful reminder that it's okay to struggle and to have moments of doubt, but that it's important to keep moving forward. Rya Hazelwood's insights are not just inspiring but practical. This book is a great roadmap for anyone looking to reignite their optimism when life feels overwhelming. It's a beautiful reminder that, no matter where you are in your journey, there's always hope, always a way forward and always the opportunity to build the life you dream of."

– Lauren Hubbard
Photographer, Resilient Optimist
& Personal Growth Enthusiast

"I love my life. But being a mom and wife – while dealing with personal medical challenges and constantly striving to create a better life for my family – hasn't always been easy. On top of that, while my work providing home care for elderly and ill individuals is deeply rewarding, the emotional toll can be heavy. This book reminded me that resilience is a journey, not a destination. Author Rya Hazelwood's message of relentless optimism resonated with me on such a deep level. It helped me stay grounded in gratitude, push through my toughest days, and embrace the belief that even when things get hard, there's always a path forward. This is the inspiration I didn't know I needed."

– Kimberly Gregory
Mother, Warrior
& Professional Caregiver

"As a former police officer, I spent years in a high-stakes, high-stress environment. I've seen and had to emotionally overcome some of the hardest things life can throw at you. Transitioning from that world into pursuing my passion as a beauty influencer has been both exhilarating and overwhelming. *Relentless Optimism & Other Life Goals* helped me rediscover my optimism when I needed it most and encouraged me to keep pushing forward, especially when doubt crept in. Rya Hazelwood's blend of practical tools and relentless optimism was like a guiding light, helping me stay grounded and motivated. No matter how tough the shift, I now believe in the power of my own story and the impact I can have, thanks to this empowering guide."

– Dipa Argano
Former Police Officer, Rising Influencer
& Pursuer of Dreams

Relentless Optimism
& OTHER LIFE GOALS

RYA HAZELWOOD

Relentless Optimism

IG@relentless.optimism.xo
www.relentlessoptimism.org

RELENTLESS OPTIMISM, LLC
Atlanta, Georgia USA
www.relentlessoptimism.org

ISBNs:
- Hardcover: 979-8-9918150-5-5
- Paperback: 979-8-9918150-1-7
- E-book: 979-8-9918150-9-3

FIRST EDITION 2024

COVER AND INTERIOR DESIGN BY RYA HAZELWOOD
Cover image by Juno_2015/Pixabay.com

Images Used Within:
- Dedication: azsudr/Pixabay.com
- Prologue: TheDigitalTeacup/Pixabay.com
- Part 1: purpleivy/Pixabay.com
- Part 2: xarkamx/Pixabay.com
- Part 3: uncredited/Pixabay.com
- Epilogue: AI/Google Gemini
- The Beginning: AI/Google Gemini

Dedication

TO MY VILLAGE

To my family, whose steadfast love, wisdom and support anchored me, and to my friends, whose help and laughter were lifelines.

You held me close, loved me in ways I never knew possible and stood by me with unwavering strength when I felt like I was falling apart. In my darkest hours, when the world seemed frayed and my faith faltered, you gently gathered my broken pieces, weaving me back together as you walked beside me toward the light.

Your guidance, grace and belief in me are gifts beyond measure.

Mom — Your love and guidance are my bedrock. Your boundless generosity of spirit means the world to me.

Kacy — Thank you for wrapping me in love and hope, and for gifting me your grace and kindness even when I felt undeserving.

Madeline — You held my hand and heart, offering exactly what I needed when I needed it most. I am forever grateful.

Dad — Your quiet strength, faith and steadfast presence are invaluable. Thank you for stepping in, without fail, every time.

Patrick & Leo — Your patience, support and generosity have lifted me up more than you know.

Lauren – You are sunshine personified. Your unwavering love and strength bolster my spirit without fail, and I am deeply grateful.

Amanda – Your wisdom and life experience were a compass guiding me through the fog. Thank you.

Kristen – I am so grateful for your friendship, strength and support.

Leigh – Your wisdom and love are roots that keep me grounded, even in the midst of the storm. Thank you for your forever friendship.

Robbie & Lucas – You are my North Stars, my guiding lights. You are the greatest blessings in my life and have taught me the true meaning of unconditional love.

Eric – Thank you for helping me reclaim my power. Your love has helped me heal, grow and rediscover who I was always meant to be.

In your own ways, you each stood as sentinels, guarding my heart as it healed and whispering truths when the lies grew loud. This book carries your imprint, etched in every word.

You helped me turn hopeless into hopeful. My relentless optimism is born of your love. And I am forever grateful.

TABLE OF CONTENTS

Introduction

BEAUTIFULLY BROKEN UNTIL
WE CHOOSE TO BE WHOLE

"You are allowed to be both a masterpiece and a work in progress, simultaneously."
   — Sophia Bush

We all carry stories of sadness and struggle, our challenges and crosses to bear. That's a universal truth. These days, being "beautifully broken" is often worn as a badge of honor, a way to embrace our scars. But at the same time, so many of us hide our pain behind tired eyes and practiced smiles. We wear resilience like a shield, taking pride in the grin-and-bear-it attitude, all while feeling isolated and alone.

So, I'm glad you picked up this book. Because if nothing else, I want you to carry this with you: **You are not alone.** Even if you set this book down after reading this sentence, let those words stay with you. You are absolutely *not* alone.

Now, you might be wondering: who am I to say this? What qualifies me to share advice or offer guidance?

Good question. I'm not a psychiatrist, psychologist nor counselor. I have no formal training in mental health or therapy. And if you are struggling, I wholeheartedly encourage you to seek professional help.

What I do have is life experience. And what I intend to do here is to share my stories – the lessons I gleaned along the path from hardship to happiness – and to be a part of your village as you navigate your own journey.

While life has thrown me plenty of curveballs, from a (very brief and easily escapable) kidnapping in Beijing to building and selling a multi-million-dollar business, my road has also been marked by two deeply personal and transformative detours: two failed marriages, each fraught with turmoil and emotional abuse.

The first relationship lasted nearly 15 years, 10 of them married, with a man we'll call "Trip." He was an alcoholic, though I didn't fully understand the depths of his addiction – or the emotional abuse that came with it – until years later. Life with him was a rollercoaster of highs and lows, hope and heartbreak.

During that time, I also underwent three years of fertility treatments, including in-vitro fertilization (IVF). It's a difficult journey in the best of circumstances, but mine was compounded by the chaos of my marriage. I was trying so hard to build a future that I couldn't see the cracks in the foundation of my present.

You might wonder: why did I stay? Why fight so hard for a child in the midst of all that turmoil?

The truth is, I was a chronic magical thinker. I clung to the belief that things would get better, that my dreams would miraculously come true. And while I'm Type A in most areas of my life, when it came to my marriage, I procrastinated. It was often easier to survive the day than to face the truth. I told myself, "It's bad now, but in five years, it will be better." Even though, deep down, I knew that in five years, it was likely to be worse.

So, I spent too long surviving until I became a shell of myself. It wasn't until I finally left that I realized just how much of myself I had lost. And I didn't know how starved I was for love and connection until I felt it again.

Which brings me to "Chad."

My second marriage began as a fairytale. He told me we were soulmates, and I believed him. I fell hard and fast, blind to the red flags. Looking back, I now see it as textbook narcissism: the love bombing, the charm, the promises. But it didn't take long for the mask to slip.

Eleven months in, I discovered Chad's first online infidelity ... or at least the first I was aware of. He swore it was meaningless, and I wanted to believe him. It wasn't until two years later, after uncovering a much more elaborate affair, that I began to rescue myself from what I now recognize as a trauma bond.

A trauma bond is insidious. It's a cycle of push and pull, give and take – positive reinforcement followed by punishment. Over time, it creates a confusing dependency and a gradual erosion of self. Even the strongest among us can be caught in its web.

I describe myself as a relentless optimist, and some people assume that means I'm bubbly all the time or only see the silver lining. But relentless optimism isn't about a Pollyanna attitude, and it's not about ignoring reality.

To me, relentless optimism is about holding onto the belief that good things are possible and being willing to work for them, even when the path is hard. As Bear Grylls once said: "Being brave isn't the absence of fear. Being brave is having that fear but finding a way through it."

It's not the absence of realism or even moments of pessimism. Rather, relentless optimism is the unwavering belief that tomorrow can be better, as long as we have the courage and will to fight for it.

Rya Hazelwood | 21

That's what this book is about: finding hope in the face of adversity; reframing your mindset; and moving from beautifully broken to strong, resilient and whole – like a remarkable mosaic forged in the flames.

It's about showing you that you are not alone and sharing the tools, guidance and stories to help you create a vision for your future and a roadmap to get there.

Thank you for joining me on this journey.

While some names and details have been changed to protect privacy, the heart of these stories remains true. I hope they remind you that while change can be daunting, it's worth it.

On the other side of hurt and fear is happiness, and it's waiting for you.

Part 1:
The First Fall

TRIP, ALCOHOLISM & MAGICAL THINKING

Chapter 1: The Slow Decline

Life is funny sometimes. You feel strong, empowered and safe. Then one day, you wake up trapped in a situation you never imagined for yourself.

The thing is, if we jumped straight from contentment to crisis, it would be easy to see all of the red flags, all of the reasons to leave. But it rarely works like that, does it? It's more like the proverbial frog in the pot of water. He gets in when the water is cool and comfortable, and as it slowly heats, he adjusts to the warmth … until suddenly, he's boiling.

That's what my failed marriages felt like. Each began with love and excitement, full of promise in their own unique ways. But over time, they slowly degraded – so gradually that I could justify each step, make excuses and grant the benefit of the doubt again and again. By the time I finally woke up to see how harmful and abusive they had become, I was already boiling.

I was born in Santa Cruz, California, to a strong, beautiful and independent woman who was putting herself through college. When I was six, she married my dad, a West Point graduate and officer in the Army.

We left California shortly thereafter when he was reassigned from Fort Ord to Fort Benning, Georgia. From there, we bounced around the southeast before landing in the suburbs of Atlanta when I was eight.

After four years in Nashville earning my B.A. from Vanderbilt University, I returned to Atlanta and began building my career.

By the time I was 25, I was living in a condo I owned in between Midtown and Downtown, working in marketing and spending my free time with friends at the many vibrant hangouts Atlanta had to offer.

That's when I met Trip, through a set of silly circumstances that started with a lost phone at Atlanta's Music Midtown festival and ended with my best friend dating his. While they only lasted a few months, it was long enough for me to meet Trip, even though he was living in Baltimore, Maryland, at the time.

At first, we spent a lot of time chatting online during the day and talking on the phone at night. He seemed smart, adventurous and cool, and I was quickly drawn in by his good looks and charm. Two months later, Trip moved to Atlanta – ostensibly to be closer to his best friend and to take advantage of the better job market for web developers.

We began dating immediately and were married five years later.

I knew he was a drinker. We'd kick off weekends with mimosas and crossword puzzles at a local brunch spot and end the day with wine or cocktails. But I was in my mid-20s, he was in his early 30s, and that's just what you did when you didn't have kids, right?

I grew out of that phase. Trip never did.

By the time our first child – let's call him "Aiden" – was born, we were living in the suburbs where we had more space, better schools and fewer bars. And Trip had slipped from heavy drinker to full-blown alcoholic.

At first, when he started passing out by 7 p.m. – sometimes on the couch, sometimes upright in a chair on the deck – I thought he was just exhausted from having a newborn and all the stress that brings. But when I started finding wine and liquor bottles hidden around the house, I knew the truth was darker. And with the drinking came an angry side of Trip I hadn't seen before.

By the time Aiden was two months old, Trip was sleeping in a separate bedroom. After a failed attempt at marriage counseling, I was talking to a divorce attorney before Aiden turned two.

"You can get a divorce," they said. "But Trip will still have your toddler for two weeks in the summer, a week during the holidays and every other weekend."

For parents who don't struggle with addiction or anger issues, this arrangement might be workable. But when your co-parent is a danger to themselves and others, it's terrifying.

I saw those times with Trip as a potential death sentence for my child. I knew he loved Aiden and didn't think he'd be intentionally violent, but I was convinced that he'd be drunk, angry and irresponsible.

"At least if we're under the same roof," I thought, "I can keep my baby safe. I can keep us insulated from Trip's drinking and anger."

And I did, to a degree. But the years that followed were a rollercoaster.

There were stretches of time — five days, two weeks, sometimes even a month — when he'd stop drinking, and I'd latch onto just enough hope to keep going. Enough hope to fuel my chronic magical thinking.

But those times were the exception, not the rule. Most days were rife with alcohol, and with his intoxication came verbal and emotional abuse. He once told me, with a twisted pride, "You can say anything you want when you're fighting," as though his venomous words were justified.

I did not subscribe to the same theory.

Suffice it to say, life felt like a constant rollercoaster, with daily battles over Trip's drinking. Each day was filled with disappointment, worry and volatility.

To the outside world, we were a picture-perfect family. Social media painted us as smiling parents with a giggly baby: a friendly, successful dad; a bubbly, outgoing mom; and a peaceful life full of love and laughter. But behind closed doors, it was anything but. Our home was turbulent, and I spent every day on edge, waiting for the next alcohol-infused tirade.

In my mind, though, I felt trapped. I wasn't going to allow Aiden to face his father's drinking and anger alone, and according to my lawyer, there were no other options.

Supervised visitation, they said, was difficult to get, and even then, it was awful for all parties, especially the child.

So, in my mind, we were stuck until Aiden turned 18. That was our future for the next 16 years. Period.

Two years later, when Aiden was four, I realized I wanted another baby. More than that, I wanted my child to have a sibling – a lifelong companion to share the bond of family. Thus, I began what turned into a three-year struggle with secondary infertility.

Chapter 2: Three-Year Delay

Trigger Warning: *This chapter and the next include my experiences with secondary infertility and pregnancy. If these are difficult topics for you, feel free to skip ahead.*

Anyone who has struggled with infertility knows the emotional and physical tolls it takes and the laser-like focus it can demand.

Every month, you track temperatures and hormones. You schedule doctor's appointments and even intimacy itself. Then comes the anxious two-week wait between possible conception and the day you can take a pregnancy test. You tell yourself to stay grounded, to manage your expectations, but it rarely works. Despite your best efforts, your mind fills with dreams of a baby.

And then your period comes. While you know, intellectually, there was no baby that cycle, your heart tells you a different story. And the sense of loss is profound and crushing.

Then you pick yourself up and do it all over again.

I did this every month for almost three years. From tears to resolve to hope and right back to tears. Rinse. Repeat.

Six months into this routine, we saw a fertility doctor, and I started oral medication. Six months later, we moved on to intrauterine insemination (IUI), which required regular doctor's visits for me and a monthly visit for Trip.

Nine IUI attempts, only three of which were viable, and about $12,000 later, we moved on to IVF.

When all was said and done, I added up the cost of the journey: $46,000, 88 doctor's visits and four minor procedures. In the final months, I was at the doctor's office every third day, including on Thanksgiving Day and Christmas Eve.

In short, trying to have a second child was all-consuming for almost three years. Tunnel vision took over. Vacations were postponed, holidays delayed and alcoholic rages, if not excused, were at least not fully dealt with. I had convinced myself that I was stuck in that marriage until the kids were old enough to leave home. So, if I wanted another baby, and if I wanted my child to have a sibling, this was my only option.

When Trip was drinking — which felt like all the time — he would yell, call me every terrible name he could think of, attack my character and fling insults with abandon. I would struggle to stay calm, to not take the bait and to not engage. I'd draw on my inner sense of self-worth — bruised and battered under his tirades — and remind myself of who I really was.

I also fell under the seductive spell of magical thinking. It allowed me to gloss over the bad, focus on the immediate goal (a baby), and picture a bright and happy, if not realistic, future for all of us.

"When the fertility journey is over, I'll focus on everything else. Trip will get better. We'll travel and live happily ever after," I told myself.

Somehow, in the fantasy I had created and clung to, Trip miraculously stopped drinking. Life magically became a picture of peace and happiness. There were no concrete plans for how this would happen, no thoughts about the effort it would require, and no acknowledgment of whether he was even willing to change. It was just a dream that one day – "poof" – like a Fairy Godmother had waved her wand, everything would be fixed.

Desperation and magical thinking can convince you of anything, reality be damned.

That said, despite the difficulty of the journey, ultimately every dollar, every fight and every tear were worth it to have my second son, "Jacob," a miracle according to my doctors in his existence and perfection.

I feel blessed beyond measure that we had the means to pursue this, and that our attempts were ultimately successful. And I hold deep empathy for anyone on their own fertility journey.

But, as will come as no surprise to anyone, a three-year delay in dealing with the reality of Trip's drinking didn't solve anything for him or for us. If anything, it got worse.

Ultimately, it was his extreme actions that forced my hand and finally led me to ask for a divorce.

Chapter 3: Beginning of the End

During my second pregnancy, Trip tried to get sober a couple of times. It would last a week or two. He'd start looking healthier, feeling better and his self-esteem would grow in the absence of alcohol. And for a brief moment, hope would blossom.

But then the drinking would start again.

Trip wasn't someone who could have a casual drink after work. If he had one drink, he wouldn't stop until he passed out. And just like that, we'd be right back to where we started.

But I was early in my pregnancy, and without the constant doctor's visits of the last few years, I started to reclaim small pieces of my life. I even took my then seven-year-old son, Aiden, on a road trip to visit family in Virginia, leaving Trip and the drama of his company behind. It was an amazing reprieve from the volatility of home.

Until I learned that, while Aiden and I were several hundred miles away, Trip, despite my protests, had purchased a handgun.

This is not a statement on any of the political issues surrounding gun ownership. It's simply a statement about a volatile, irresponsible alcoholic having a gun in a house with a small child and a pregnant wife. My worst fear was that he would get drunk, take out the gun and accidentally – or intentionally – fire it.

And my worst fear would eventually be realized.

Over the course of my pregnancy, things went from bad to worse.

Trip would get drunk and wander our suburban neighborhood at night, crashing parties and alarming our neighbors. These incidents strained our relationships with them and resulted in one drunk-and-disorderly arrest.

He was ordered to attend limited counseling and prescribed anti-anxiety medication. While the medication briefly lengthened the fuse on his hair-trigger anger, it ultimately became just another substance for him to abuse. The counselor failed to identify his addiction, and Trip's court-ordered visits came and went with no meaningful changes.

Meanwhile, I clung to magical thinking. Six months into my pregnancy, I even planned and paid for a week at Disney World, scheduled for the end of my maternity leave. We hadn't traveled in years because of the fertility journey, and I desperately wanted to create a happy memory for Aiden, who had just turned eight.

Jacob was born in early July. Laboring all day turned into a race to the delivery room. He arrived under the care of an expert doctor and midwife before the hospital staff even had time to register my name. But he was here, and he was perfect!

Those first days should have been peaceful and filled with joy. My baby was healthy, and we were in the insulated environment of the hospital. But looking back, I recognize that time as the true and final beginning of the end.

The day we were supposed to go home is a day I will never forget — for all the wrong reasons.

The plan was simple. Trip would pick Aiden up from day camp at 4 p.m., then drive to the hospital in my car, already prepared with an installed car seat, to take Jacob and me home.

I started to worry when I hadn't heard from Trip by 4:30. Then by 5:00, with no calls, texts or sign of them, panic began to set in.

I called the day camp. Aiden was still there. Thankfully, they had an aftercare program until 6 p.m., so he was safe.

I called my mom. She was stuck in traffic, but she assured me that she would head straight to the camp, pick up Aiden and then come to get Jacob and me.

Worried that my mom wouldn't make it in time, I called my friend Lauren, who worked closer. She immediately dropped her plans, picked up Aiden, playing soccer with him in the parking lot until my mom arrived.

With Aiden in tow, my mom went first to my house. And what she found was alarming.

Trip's car was in the driveway with the windows down and the driver's side door ajar. The front door to the house was wide open, and it was dark inside.

She found Trip sitting on the couch, nonchalant.

"What are you doing?" she asked. "Are you ok?"

"Yes," he replied slowly. "I'm fine."

"Weren't you supposed to pick up Aiden, Rya and Jacob?" she pressed, knowing full well he was.

"No," he replied.

"Have you talked to Rya?" she asked, knowing that he had not.

"Yes. Everything is fine," he repeated, dazed.

The open prescription container and empty wine bottles told a different story.

Locating the keys to my car and closing the front door, my mom and Aiden left the father of my children sitting there in the dark and drove to the hospital to pick us up.

While I waited, my nurse came in with words of encouragement. She handed me the paperwork for Jacob's birth certificate, which I filled out alone, making the final decisions on his first and middle names by myself.

It was in that quiet, sterile room that I finally acknowledged the truth I had been avoiding: no amount of wishing or magical thinking would ever change my reality. Not in five years. Not when the kids were older.

I sat there, firm – if nervous – in the knowledge that if I wanted my life to change, I was going to have to change it myself.

I set a boundary with Trip: no more excuses, no more drinking or no more family.

Between July 5 and August 10 that summer, Trip crossed that line so many times that I finally kicked him out and took the necessary, permanent steps to protect my children and myself.

By the time we divorced, there were enough incidents on record that the parenting plan ordered by the judge only allowed Trip to have Aiden from 10 a.m. to 6 p.m. every other Saturday. No weekends, no overnights. And Jacob wouldn't start spending time with Trip alone until he was three years old.

It wasn't perfect, but it was the most protective arrangement I could get.

Chapter 4: Daily Trials

While it had been going on for years, I never fully adjusted to the almost daily trials of living with an alcoholic in the full throes of the disease.

Every day, I stumbled upon the evidence: beer cans, wine bottles and flasks hidden behind window curtains, lined up behind his computer screen or stashed in his car. Sprite bottles weren't safe – they were often just a disguise for vodka. Quick trips to the store for milk frequently ended with hundreds of dollars mysteriously spent. (Of course, the explanation was booze.)

Trip could go from seemingly sober to stumbling drunk in an instant. It was both alarming and exhausting.

I'd wake up in the middle of the night to crashes and bangs. I found him passed out on the stairs, sprawled on the couch covered in spaghetti, or face down on the floor. Some nights, I'd discover gas stove burners left on, unattended and dangerous. Other nights, I'd find only an empty house as he wandered off on his late-night escapades.

Watching this happen day after day was like witnessing a slow-motion collapse – an agonizing decline from the confident, intelligent man I had once known to a hollow shell of himself.

I believe Trip's alcoholism was, in many ways, an expression of self-loathing. But it didn't stop there. The disease also warped his mind in ways that were both significant and terrifying.

One night, he woke me up and insisted that I come downstairs. He was convinced that he had discovered how to control a ball of energy, that he could harness "the force" like some kind of real-life Jedi.

So there I was, standing on our deck in pajamas at 11:30 p.m., watching the man I had once dreamed of building a life with, waving his hands in the air. He was so certain he could summon and manipulate this invisible energy.

When nothing happened, frustration and confusion etched themselves across his face.

"I was just doing it!" he said, visibly upset.

And my fear and worry hit me like a tidal wave.

When I reflect on my life with Trip, there are three moments that stand out as particularly terrifying. This is one of them. The second involved his gun. The third came the last night he spent in our home.

Chapter 5: It's Not Boring

Life with an alcoholic isn't boring.

It's stressful, scary and sad. It's filled with worry, desperation and heartbreak ... but boring it is not.

You go to sleep praying for a peaceful night, uncertain of what might come in those dark hours when you are at your most vulnerable. Sometimes, by some miracle, you sleep until morning. But more often than not, there's a disruption in one form or another.

Have you ever been woken up by a police officer inside of your home? I have.

One night, I woke to the sound of a voice I didn't recognize calling up the stairs. Groggy and disoriented, I stepped out of my bedroom to find a policeman standing at the bottom of the staircase, looking up at me respectfully. His alert eyes took in my pajamas and sleep-ridden face, no doubt assessing whether I, too, was intoxicated – I wasn't – or if I could be trusted to care for the child he knew lived there.

He asked me to follow him outside.

When I stepped onto the driveway, I saw a firetruck, a group of firefighters and a gaggle of curious neighbors gathered in the late-night darkness.

It was past midnight, and while Aiden and I slept, Trip had gone on one of his alcohol-infused walks, fallen and hit his head hard enough to break the skin, which, as head wounds tend to do, bled profusely.

A fireman handed me the leash of my startled dog, explained that they had administered first aid and then sent Trip to the emergency room in an ambulance.

It was the night before Aiden's fifth birthday party.

Standing in my driveway, holding the leash and holding myself together, I tried to ignore the prying eyes of the strangers who shared my street. I couldn't help but wonder: why were so many of them awake? Why had they chosen to gather and gawk? And how had I become the neighborhood spectacle?

Not knowing the severity of Trip's injury, I was torn. Should I rush to the hospital to be by his side? Or should I stay home, let him handle the mess he'd created and wait for his return?

I was exhausted – burnt out on the dramatics – but I still felt obligated to do the right thing.

So, I called my mom. In the middle of the night, I called my mom, and she came over, just in case. Just in case I needed to leave the house so Aiden could sleep. Just in case it didn't turn out okay. Just in case it did.

Just in case.

Next, I called the ER. The operator transferred me to Trip's nurse, who made her exasperation abundantly clear the moment she answered the phone. I could only imagine how drunk and dramatic Trip must have been for her patience to wear so thin.

Though she wouldn't answer my questions, she handed the phone to Trip. "I'm having brain surgery!" he cried. "My brain is coming out of my head!"

And that's when I knew the injury was minor.

When Trip arrived home the next morning in a sad and prideful taxicab, hungover and tired, he had two staples and a bandage on his head.

When we left for Aiden's birthday party a few hours later, Trip had a lunchbox full of beer.

But this wasn't even the most dramatic way I've been woken up in the middle of the night.

Chapter 6: Shots Fired

I mentioned earlier that there are three terrifying moments that stand out to me when I think about my time with Trip. This is the second one.

In hindsight, allowing Trip to keep a gun in the house was one of my gravest mistakes. I knew it was a terrible idea. I argued against it, I protested, but eventually, I gave in. At that time, I was already so exhausted from the endless battles over his drinking and behavior that I didn't have the energy for yet another fight.

He had promised me the gun would stay locked in a small handgun safe, which would be stored in the attic. But I should have known better than to trust his promises.

The gun terrified me. It was a dangerous weapon in a house with a small child and an unpredictable alcoholic. And one night, my worst fear came true.

It was 2:36 a.m. when I bolted upright in bed, heart pounding before my conscious mind caught up. A gunshot! That was a gunshot, and it was close.

At the time, I was pregnant with Jacob. We were fine. My first instinct was to check on Aiden. I found him sound asleep, uninjured and unaware of what had just happened. I moved him into my bedroom before making my way downstairs, pulse pounding in my ears.

I found Trip standing on the porch, gun in hand, his eyes glazed and his movements unsteady. The dog sat by his side, clearly alarmed but loyal nonetheless.

"What did you do?" I demanded, my voice trembling with a mix of fear and fury.

"I accidentally fired into the ground," he said, leaning against the railing. The stench of alcohol clung to him like a second skin.

I hoped he was telling the truth. From what I could see, there were no lights on in the neighborhood, no signs of distress. It didn't appear anyone had been injured. And I was determined to make sure it stayed that way.

I don't know how I mustered the courage, but I took the gun from his hands. Terrified and unfamiliar with firearms, I held it gingerly, acutely aware of the very real danger it posed. I took it and the dog and went inside.

I collected the small gun safe, placed the gun inside of it, and locked it, myself and Aiden in my bedroom, securing us all for the rest of the night.

As I sat there, the weight of the situation crashed down on me. I texted my dad, begging him to come get the gun. Though he was out of town, he arranged for his friend Pete to retrieve it the next morning.

Pete arrived at 10 a.m., his face grim as I handed him the safe. He gave a warning glance to Trip, who now sober, was skulking in the background. Pete opened the safe, removed the magazine and cleared the chamber.

"There was a bullet ready to be fired," Pete stated, confirming my fear. I felt a wave of relief knowing the weapon was out of my house and no longer in Trip's possession.

Placing the weapon back in its portable safe, Pete took it home with him, later handing it over to my father.

I'll forever be grateful to Pete and my dad for removing the gun that day.

Trip's story changed a couple of times as he tried to justify what he did. But his explanations went from bad to worse. First it was an accident. Then he was just testing it. Then, he saw people running through the woods behind our house with a stolen TV – a complete fabrication – and he thought that was cause to fire at them.

What I believe is that he was drunk and wanted to feel powerful, and he shot the gun into the yard.

For days afterward, I couldn't stop imagining what could have happened.

What if Trip had aimed differently? What if Aiden had wandered downstairs? What if I hadn't woken up when I did?

The "what ifs" were endless and terrifying.

So, I made a promise to myself: no matter what, the gun would never come back into our house. I had already insisted it stay locked away, but now I was done making concessions. The moment Trip pulled that trigger, it became non-negotiable.

Still, even with the gun gone, the fear didn't leave me. A deep, gnawing unease clung to me, impossible to shake. I knew how close we had come to tragedy. And yet, instead of leaving, I rationalized. I told myself everything would be fine now that the gun was gone.

I wish I could tell you that that was the final straw. But as anyone who's lived through a toxic relationship knows, these moments don't happen all at once. They build up, layer by layer, until the truth becomes undeniable.

While the timeline accelerated after the incident with the gun – in fact, my divorce from Trip was finalized just five months after Jacob was born – the reality was that the marriage had been unraveling for years.

During those years, I tried everything I could think of to open Trip's eyes to what he was doing.

I'd wait until he was sober and try to have rational conversations.

I wrote him letters and emails, pouring out my fears and frustrations.

I recounted the reckless things he did while blacked out, hoping to hold up a mirror so he could see the danger.

I appealed to him as the father of our children, begging him to think about their future.

I pointed out how closely his path mirrored that of his mother, who had suffered from the same disease.

I lined up the empty bottles I found hidden around the house, hoping the alarming quantity would wake him up.

I even asked his family for help, though they were hundreds of miles away and we were not close. But I was desperate and didn't know what else to do.

Trip's dad came down from Maryland once, promising to have a heart-to-heart with him and drag him to an Alcoholics Anonymous meeting. But nothing came of it.

When I asked for help again, his family's response was cold and dismissive: "You married him; he's your problem."

In the end, the people who stood by me were my own family. My mother, especially, was my rock. I leaned on her constantly, and I can't imagine what it would have been like to go through that alone.

Their support gave me the strength to hold on, for myself and especially for my children, until I was ready to break free from the rollercoaster for good.

Chapter 7: Enough is a Feeling Not an Amount

I remember the day vividly.

I was home with my eight-year-old son and my not-quite-two-month-old baby, trying to maintain some semblance of normalcy amid the chaos.

Trip had recently been charged with his second DUI. That morning, he left for an AA meeting, returning a couple of hours later full of positivity. He spoke highly of the men he'd met, the impact of the meeting and his renewed commitment to sobriety.

What I didn't know then was that he had also returned with a box full of wine and liquor in the trunk of his car.

A week earlier, after years of broken promises, countless ultimatums, and lines in the sand that had been pushed back again and again, I had finally set a hard boundary. I told him, in no uncertain terms: if he drank again, it was over.

There would be no more chances.

That night, Trip couldn't hide his intoxication, and I reached my breaking point. I had finally had enough.

After the kids were asleep, I confronted him. Calmly but firmly, I told him that in the morning, he would need to leave.

That's when he reached for his car keys.

Fearing for his safety and the safety of others, I grabbed the keys first. I told him I would return them in the morning and turned to go upstairs.

But before I could make it even halfway, he grabbed me on the stairs. What followed was the only physical altercation I've ever experienced.

Bruised and terrified, still clutching the keys in my shaking hand, I made it to my bedroom and locked the door behind me. Inside, my two children were asleep, blissfully unaware of the chaos that had unfolded just outside the door.

That was the last night Trip ever slept in our house, the home we had shared for eight years.

Three months later, our divorce was finalized.

Trip was dead within a year, claimed by the very disease he had refused to fight.

Chapter 8: The Phone Call

I learned about Trip's death over the phone from a police officer while the boys and I were out of town on vacation. His family had known for days, yet they allowed me to hear about the death of my children's father – a man I had once loved, and for a time, thought I would spend my life with – from a stranger.

In that moment, shock collided with grief, anger and confusion. How could they not have told me? And how was I going to explain this devastating loss to my children?

In hindsight, perhaps it shouldn't have been surprising, given how they engaged during our marriage and what they chose to do after Trip's death.

By the time I found out that Trip's dad and stepmom had even come to Atlanta, they had already left town.

They had traveled in from Maryland, spent a weekend sorting through Trip's belongings and then disappeared without a word. There was no advance notice, no outreach while they were in town, not even a call to check on their grandchildren.

Instead, they spent their time sorting, selling and shipping Trip's possessions. With an estate intestate, what should have gone to his sons – Aiden, who was nine at the time, and Jacob, just one – was taken by his father and stepmother.

They disposed of what they didn't want, sold what they could and sent the rest to themselves and Trip's sister, including Trip's paid-off car.

They left nothing for Aiden and Jacob. No wristwatch, no ballcap, nothing of value sentimental or otherwise.

The only remembrances my boys have of their father are the photographs I took throughout our relationship and the few items he left behind when he moved out of our home: an acoustic guitar, a pocket watch and his wedding band.

We've had no contact with his family since. Instead of embracing Aiden and Jacob, they choose to act as if we don't exist.

Then again, perhaps I should have seen it coming. They turned a blind eye to Trip's drinking during his life – why should I have expected them to show up for my boys after his death?

Chapter 9: Prelude to Part 2 – Tactics

I wouldn't wish abuse on anyone, whether physical or emotional. Both leave lasting scars, visible or not, and both can profoundly impact your sense of self.

That said, physical abuse is often easier to identify. When someone physically harms you, there's little room for doubt: a bruise, a cut, a broken bone – they're tangible, undeniable.

Emotional abuse is different. It's insidious. Subtle. Harder to label. It sneaks up on you, eroding your confidence, making you question your worth and your perception of reality. It's the kind of abuse that whispers, "Maybe it's not that bad," or, worse, "Maybe this is your fault."

My experiences with abuse have been emotional.

With Trip, the abuse came in the form of anger. He wielded his words like weapons, hurling insults and accusations designed to cut deep. He would call me vile names, belittle my character, and then rationalize it later as something you're "allowed to do" when you're angry.

He took a twisted pride in the venom he could unleash.

With Chad, my second husband, the emotional abuse was more calculated, more nefarious and ultimately, more damaging.

Trip's goal was to hurt me with his words. With Chad, it felt different. Looking back, I believe hurting me was not his primary goal; rather, he wanted to control me.

Pain was just one of the many tactics in his arsenal.

Part 2:
Shattered Illusions

NARCISSISM, EMOTIONAL
ABUSE & INFIDELITY

Chapter 10: Into the Fire

Out of the pot of boiling water and into the fire …

Author's Note: The experiences and reflections shared in this section are based on my personal memories and observations. Recountings of emails, messages and other communications are drawn from my recollection of materials that Chad voluntarily shared with me in his efforts to demonstrate transparency and seek reconciliation. While I have strived to present events accurately as I remember them, I acknowledge that others may have differing perspectives or interpretations.

When I met Chad, I didn't yet understand what true narcissism looked like. I didn't know people could behave, think or treat others in such a toxic way. Over the nearly four years we were together I got a masterclass in the Narcissist's Playbook, though I didn't recognize it as such at the time.

If you suspect you might be involved with a narcissist – whether romantically, professionally or even within your family or friend circle – there are countless resources available to help you understand what that looks like and how to protect yourself. Therapists who specialize in helping people recover from the trauma of these relationships can be especially valuable. If you're navigating something similar, I encourage you to seek support.

I shared the analogy of the frog in the pot when talking about my marriage to Trip. It applies here too, only magnified.

Abuse doesn't come crashing in all at once; it creeps. It starts small and subtly, disguised as warmth. The water moves from cool to warm, and you adjust. Then it gets a little hotter, and you adjust again.

Their behavior becomes more toxic, but it happens so gradually that you don't recognize it for what it is. Yellow, orange and eventually red flags pop up one by one, but because they show up slowly, you find ways to explain them away.

You give the benefit of the doubt again and again – because that's what you do for someone you love, right? And if they love you, as they say they do, surely they have your best interests at heart.

You tell yourself it was wonderful before, it can be wonderful again. And you've already invested so much …

You stay, not because you don't see the problems, but because fear and magical thinking convince you that this time, it will be different.

Before you know it, you're trapped in a web of lies, excuses and a trauma bond so tightly woven that escaping feels impossible.

In writing this book, I've had to confront the shame I was carrying about how I "allowed" myself to be treated – the lies I believed, the behavior I tolerated and the times I stayed when I should have left.

I consider myself strong and intelligent. And yet, I fell into that trap. I stayed, over and over again.

But here's the thing: that shame is misplaced. And it's how so many victims end up blaming themselves for staying in an abusive situation. When you're in the middle of it – in the storm of manipulation and confusion – it doesn't feel black and white. It's not *always* bad; in fact, it may not even be *usually* bad. That's part of what makes it so difficult to leave.

It's a vicious cycle, layered with mixed feelings and trauma-bonded self-doubt.

When I met Chad, I was confident, capable and successful. I was the kind of person people gravitated toward. I was smart, emotionally intelligent and deeply loving.

And here's the truth: while society sometimes paints the victims of abuse as weak, narcissists and abusers often target strong people. They align themselves with those who have qualities they admire or envy, traits they wish they possessed.

And in a cruel twist, those very strengths, talents and characteristics that first attracted them are often the ones they'll later try to undermine and destroy.

What I remind myself of now – and what I encourage you to keep in mind if you see yourself in these pages – is that being a victim is nothing to be ashamed of. It's not your fault. Help is available, and recovery is absolutely possible.

Chapter 11: A Mask of a Man

With Chad, the beginning seemed like a magical fairytale. What I didn't know then, but would later learn, is that those early days were not built on genuine love or connection. Instead, they were part of a carefully orchestrated manipulation tactic called love bombing.

When we met, I was vulnerable and starved for attention. Chad was charming, exciting and persistent. Everything seemed to click. I felt seen and understood in ways I hadn't felt before. I felt adored. Terms like "meant to be" and "soulmates" felt tangible and real. And how lucky was I?

The first days were filled with romantic gestures and constant affirmations. We uncovered shared interests and dreams. He told me how special I was, how unique our connection was. Days were filled with banter, compliments and his near-constant communication: texts, phone calls and in-person visits.

At the time, it all felt good. After years of loneliness with Trip, I felt valued. I felt treasured. I felt cherished.

How drastically that would change.

What I thought was the start of a loving partnership was actually what I see now to be the opening act of an insecure man trying to elevate his own social and financial status by latching onto me.

In hindsight, I see that his attention wasn't based on love. It was a tidal wave of love bombing, bulldozing boundaries and creating dependence. I don't believe he loved me then, or ever. I'm not even sure he knows what love is.

In those heady first few months, he wasn't showing me his true self. He was mirroring me, pretending to be my perfect match, while showering me with compliments and affection. He didn't give me – nor did I, naïve and unwise to the dating world, demand – the space and separation that are crucial early in a relationship. There was no breathing room to evaluate who he really was or what we were stepping into.

It seems to me now that Chad was creating a facade, a fairytale that he could use to manipulate and control me.

At some point with a narcissist, the person they once idealized topples off the pedestal they built. The love bombing ends, and devaluation begins. Emotional abuse, and for some, physical abuse, slowly becomes more overt and more frequent. By the time this happens, the trauma bond is firmly in place. Confusion and self-doubt have taken hold. A toxic cycle forms and breaking free feels nearly impossible.

Chad wore his false mask just long enough to get me deeply invested in him and the relationship. He created an environment where I – a strong, capable woman

supported by an amazing circle of friends and family —
felt isolated, dependent and desperate.

From the start, Chad's lies were pervasive. He said we
were the same age, but he was actually several years
older. He claimed to be a VP of marketing, but he was
really a mid-level salesman. He told me he owned a four-
bedroom lake house in a posh suburb and a condo
downtown. The truth? He was leasing a condo in a
questionable part of town, and subletting it to a stranger,
while renting a modest house backing up to a pond on
the outskirts of a less desirable suburb.

None of those things would have been deal breakers.
The problem was the lies.

Looking back, the deception never stopped. Chad
seemed to live in a fabricated world, desperate to
present himself as someone he wasn't.

Over time, I realized that Chad didn't see me as a partner
to love and cherish. He saw me as a way to elevate
himself.

To him, I was a Vanderbilt-educated single mother with
financial security, career success and a network that
could help him climb higher. What I viewed as middle-
class stability, he saw as an opportunity to appear
successful, like a man on the rise.

At first, he basked in my accomplishments. But as his envy grew, he began to resent the very traits that had drawn him to me.

What I've since learned is that narcissists are often attracted to strong, capable people, not because they admire those traits, but because they envy them. Instead of celebrating their partner's strengths, they seek to tear them down, piece by piece, to regain control.

Chad leveraged every kindness I showed him to his own advantage. Over the course of our short marriage, he transformed himself from an overweight salesman with a car registered in his ex-girlfriend's name to a fit business owner driving a high-end luxury brand vehicle.

But it wasn't success he earned himself. It was built on my resources, my hard work and, as I later discovered, weight loss drugs.

Now I see that what Chad wanted wasn't a partnership. He wanted a mask. He wanted me to help him construct the image of a man he could never actually be. To him, "love" wasn't a connection. It was a tool, just another tactic to keep me invested, isolated and, ultimately, trapped.

Chapter 12: Victim of the Moment

While Chad's ego felt as fragile as any narcissist's, his bravado and vanity seemed boundless.

Early in our relationship, I discovered he was taking both weight loss and muscle enhancing drugs: a revelation that came when I found a drawer full of vials during one of his failed trips to New Zealand (more on that later). When I confronted him, he brushed it off, claiming expertise in their use. Within our first year together, his weight dropped by 100 pounds.

But he didn't stop there. Chad underwent two rounds of aesthetic surgery. He poured thousands into enhancement drugs, face fillers and hair dye, seemingly in a relentless quest to remake himself.

At the time, I tried to rationalize it. Maybe he'd feel better about himself if he liked what he saw in the mirror. "Look good, feel good," I told myself.

But in hindsight, I can't help but wonder: how much of it was really for him? And how much of it was a bid to impress someone else – the "Becky" I would later discover waiting for him on the other side of a computer screen?

Throughout our short marriage, Chad also took full advantage of my health insurance and my willingness to care for him. Over the course of two years, he had three elective surgeries.

While all technically outpatient, the last one did require an overnight at the hospital. He was supposed to return home the next morning, sticking to a liquid diet while he healed.

Instead, it spiraled into a weeklong hospital stay.

From the moment he woke up from the surgery, Chad complained of severe pain, convincing his surgeon to extend his stay and even perform a secondary, exploratory procedure.

At the time, I was genuinely worried about his suffering. But now, I wonder how much of it was exaggerated – or even orchestrated.

Ignoring doctor's orders, Chad managed to charm the hospital's sweet food service attendant into sneaking sandwiches onto his lunch tray, despite the clear risks to his recovery. His behavior was reckless but deliberate, a pattern I was only beginning to recognize.

When he wasn't complaining about discomfort, he was glued to his phone, scrolling through social media and exchanging messages with women. Additionally, he seemed to thrive on the nurses' attention, though they didn't share his enthusiasm.

Later, one of them told me about his odd, attention-seeking behavior. The most bizarre instance? Just days post a procedure which required four small incisions in his abdomen, Chad attempted to do crunches on the hospital floor. Inevitably, he tore his stitches, worsening his pain and prolonging his stay.

In the moment, I chalked it up to poor judgment. But months later, when I stumbled upon a flurry of messages between him and an online flirtation, the pieces began to fall into place.

Those crunches weren't a misguided choice for his health. They were prep work – for a very specific selfie he intended to send.

Several months later, after I had asked for a divorce, Chad would, at odd times, hand me his computer or phone, claiming repentance and transparency. In what felt like an awkward and performative display of trust, I would scroll through emails, photos and messages, absorbing the fresh sting of betrayal each time.

It was during one of those instances that this memory resurfaced – of his crunches on the hospital floor. The details came flooding back as I stumbled upon a random exchange, one Chad had left in plain view as part of his so-called transparency. The messages went something like this:

A woman had messaged him, asking how he was recovering.

"Hangin' in there," he replied, casting himself as the resilient hero.

"You sure?" she asked, playing into his narrative.

"Been worse," he said, underscoring his supposed toughness.

"It was a laparoscopic, right?" she questioned, skeptical but intrigued.

"Had to go under twice," he replied dramatically.

Then came the photo: a chest-down nude, strategically framed to highlight bandages – and more.

"That's the oddest c*ck pic I've ever seen," she responded, seemingly more taken aback than impressed.

Unfazed, Chad dismissed the picture as an "accident." As though anyone could accidentally angle a camera just so, after doing crunches on a hospital room floor.

And yet, the flirtation continued, with plans discussed for a fantasy rendezvous in that woman's home country, thousands of miles away.

Even though I wasn't privy to this exchange until months after it took place, it was just one of countless examples of Chad's disloyalty and need for validation from strangers online.

By the time I saw it, I was already working to end our marriage. Yet each new revelation cut deep, reopening wounds I thought were beginning to heal.

Looking back now, I can clearly see how Chad's need for constant affirmation and attention fueled every aspect of his behavior, from the love bombing that initially swept me off my feet to the lies and betrayals that ultimately unraveled everything.

What began as a whirlwind romance had devolved into a relationship built on deception and manipulation, leaving me to piece together the truth from the fragments of his lies.

But with each new discovery, I also grew stronger and more determined to move forward. Chad's mask had slipped, and I was growing in my ability to see him – and, more importantly, myself – with a clarity I hadn't had before.

Chapter 13: Hypocritical & Unforgivable

It was a little over three years from the day Chad and I were married until the day we signed divorce papers. In that time, unbeknownst to me until close to the end, Chad likely never deleted his dating apps, spent tens of thousands of dollars on other women, proposed to an online girlfriend halfway across the world – without ever meeting her in person or even video chatting – and planned at least three solo trips from the U.S. to New Zealand "to find himself." In reality, these trips were intended to meet his online fiancée, though the COVID-19 pandemic prevented all but the final one.

Under the guise of "discipline," Chad was also emotionally abusive to my son, Aiden, who grew from eight to 12 years old during our relationship.

At first, Chad seemed like a loving stepfather. He spent afternoons playing Xbox with Aiden and even taught him to ride a bike. But as soon as he began devaluing me, he started devaluing Aiden too.

Chad claimed he was "correcting" the so-called weakness I had supposedly allowed in my son through "soft" parenting. He insisted his harshness was meant to shape Aiden into a stronger, better person.

Of all the painful memories I carry, Chad's treatment of Aiden weighs heaviest on me. I intervened every time, but it was never enough.

Hindsight can be a cruel teacher, and looking back, I wish I had left the very first time Chad displayed that kind of unforgivable behavior.

But as anyone who has lived through manipulation and gaslighting knows, it's never that simple. You want to believe the person you love, and you convince yourself that their intentions are good.

I learned the hard way that sometimes, hope and the benefit of the doubt are dangerous things.

In hindsight, the disparity in how Chad treated my two children wasn't just painful and problematic; it was revealing. His warmth toward Jacob now seems calculated, a way to maintain the illusion of being a doting father figure. His harshness toward Aiden was the other side of the coin, a cruel attempt to assert dominance and control.

With younger Jacob – too young to see through any games or narcissistic ploys, readily loving and affectionate – Chad was doting and fatherly, lavishing him with gifts and treats.

With Aiden – who was old enough to recognize the cracks in Chad's mask – he became a harsh disciplinarian, often angry and cutting under the pretense of building his character.

Aiden was intelligent, respectful and kind. He was also thoughtful and introspective, and, like many kids his age, cautious in new situations.

One evening, when Aiden was 10, he was making a pizza. When it came time to take it out of the hot oven, he hesitated, afraid he might get burned.

"Let's do it together," I said, getting up to help him.

But Chad stopped me. "Sit down," he said firmly. "He needs to do this himself."

Aiden froze, his anxiety mounting. Chad's tone shifted quickly, becoming sharper and colder. "Just reach in and take it out of the oven. Do it now, or your pizza will burn, and I'll be unhappy."

When Aiden started to cry, Chad's anger flared. Standing over him, this large man yelled at my child, trying to shame him into compliance.

I stepped in immediately, putting myself between them and ordering Chad to stop. But my intervention only fueled his indignation.

"You're undermining me!" he shouted. "You're ruining any chance I have to help Aiden grow up strong. You're the problem!"

Then came his most cutting remark: "I hate weakness."

His words hung heavy in the air, planting seeds of doubt. Was I really too soft? Was I setting Aiden up for failure by stepping in? Or was Chad simply being cruel? These questions gnawed at me.

Chad insisted his harshness was love. "What I'm doing is hard now, but it's the best thing for him in the long run. If I didn't care, I wouldn't even try."

It was gaslighting at its finest: twisting cruelty into an act of care.

After moments like these, Chad would retreat, locking himself in our bedroom for hours or even days. He claimed he needed to "cool down," but it was clear his silence was a weapon, a deliberate punishment designed to control and manipulate me.

These cycles – the cruelty toward Aiden or me, my attempts to stand up for us and the subsequent stonewalling – repeated far too often. Yet each time, Chad would emerge again, acting loving, dropping breadcrumbs of affection as if to remind me of the man I thought I had married.

And each time, I told myself it would get better. I wanted to believe in the version of Chad I had fallen for … the version he dangled in front of us during those brief respites. But it never got better in a lasting or meaningful way. Instead, the pattern only deepened, leaving me to carry the heavy weight of regret and guilt for not leaving sooner.

What Chad did to Aiden was hypocritical and unforgivable. I will never stop working to heal those wounds, both in myself and in my son. And I will never again put myself or my children in a position where we are at the mercy of someone else's cruelty.

Chapter 14: Gaslighting & Manipulation

Gaslighting is a tactic where an abuser distorts reality to make the victim question their own perception. A gaslighter might accuse their target of lying, dismiss their concerns or even label them as "crazy," all while insisting that they alone hold the truth. Over time, the victim begins to doubt their reality, becoming increasingly dependent on the abuser to define what is "real."

Manipulation works in a similar vein. Manipulators aim to influence their target's emotions or actions to serve their own interests. They might lie, criticize or exploit insecurities, all with the goal of undermining their victim's confidence and gaining control.

When you're in the thick of being repeatedly gaslit and manipulated, it's nearly impossible to see clearly. What's obvious from the outside becomes a foggy, confusing haze when you're living it.

I now know the truth: Chad never truly loved me or my son Aiden. He may not even love himself. But at the time, I believed he cared. I believed he was intelligent and intuitive. I believed he had our best interests at heart. When he told me I was failing as a parent by coddling Aiden, I doubted myself. I trusted his assessment over my own instincts.

That's what makes gaslighting and manipulation so effective: they prey on your deepest fears and self-doubts. And as a mother, I had plenty.

Like so many parents, I want to do everything in my power to give my children love, stability and the tools they need to thrive. I carried guilt about the turbulence Aiden had already lived through with Trip. I wanted to ensure he had the best chance for a happy, successful life. And I knew that sometimes, that meant doing hard things in the short term for long-term gain.

Chad leaned into that guilt, twisting it to make me doubt my instincts, to make me feel like I was failing Aiden. He convinced me that I was too soft, that only his approach could help Aiden grow up strong.

It was my first clear glimpse of Chad's manipulation, the first one I began to break free from. But it wasn't easy, and it wasn't immediate.

At the same time, I was afraid of the fallout from confronting him on most issues. The stonewalling, the outbursts of anger, the cold, calculated silences – all of these methods worked to make me shrink from confrontation. And I knew from experience that addressing problems with Chad wouldn't lead to real change anyway; it would only intensify the punishment.

Still, I couldn't ignore everything. Two issues I couldn't let go of were his treatment of Aiden and his inappropriate interactions with other women.

"What are these messages on your Facebook post?" I asked one day, having come across an overly flirtatious public exchange between Chad and a woman I did not know.

"What?" he scoffed. "That's nothing. Social media isn't real."

"It makes me uncomfortable," I said, trying to keep my tone calm and reasonable.

"You're overreacting," he snapped. "It's just Facebook."

"But I'm your wife, and it feels disrespectful. Can you delete those messages and stop flirting with other women?" I pressed, standing my ground.

"Oh God!" he exploded. "You're so sensitive and insecure. I can't be with someone who's insecure."

This was gaslighting in action – effective because it made me question myself. Instead of focusing on his behavior, I began to wonder: Am I too sensitive? Is this a problem with me?

In my effort to be a good partner, I inadvertently allowed myself to be blind to the bigger picture. In a healthy relationship, you're supposed to reflect on your own behavior and stay open to self-improvement, right? But the problem was, this wasn't a healthy relationship. I was the only one trying to grow. Chad wasn't looking for a partnership; he was looking for control.

The proverbial water kept getting hotter, but immersed in the pot, I could only see a few bubbles. I didn't recognize I was nearing a boil.

I clung to magical thinking, comforting myself with hopes of a better future. "When Chad works through his depression … when our business grows … when the kids are older …" I focused on the potential of what could be instead of facing the reality of what was.

But eventually, even that wasn't enough to quiet my inner alarm.

It took far too long — I'll admit that freely — but in January 2022, the truth became impossible to ignore. Chad's ongoing affair was exposed, shattering the illusion and piercing through the fog. There was no excusing it, no "benefit of the doubt" left to give.

It was the catalyst I needed, the final push to find the strength to leave. Enough was enough.

Chapter 15: If It Hadn't Been So Painful, It Would Have Been Funny

It's astonishing how surreal betrayal can feel when it's tangled with absurdity.

In early January, I stumbled upon the truth about Chad's affair, though "affair" feels like a woefully inadequate term. This wasn't a passing indiscretion; it was a sprawling, fabricated double life. Chad wasn't just cheating. He was engaged to someone else – planning a wedding with a woman he'd never even met in person.

More than half of our marriage had been spent in this emotional affair. Every night, while I believed he was decompressing in his car, "listening to music," he was actually on the phone with her. He sent extravagant gifts – Tiffany, Manolo Blahnik, Prada – to this woman across the world.

The crown jewel of his betrayal, however, was something I discovered while putting away laundry. Tucked away in his sock drawer, I found a $20,000, three-carat diamond engagement ring – one ring size larger than mine.

For me, he had chosen a $50 cubic zirconia ring from a TV shopping channel.

The emotional whiplash of that discovery still stings. I debated what to do. Should I take the ring? Replace it with a fake? Hide it? My lawyer cautioned against acting rashly, so ultimately, I left it where it was. Still, I couldn't help but imagine all the karmic consequences that ring might carry.

When Chad left for the airport on his final "soul-searching" trip to New Zealand – the one I knew was really about meeting her – I checked the drawer. The ring was still there. I couldn't believe it. Had he really forgotten such a significant item?

Forty-five minutes later, he burst through the door, frantic, mumbling about forgetting his watch. The lie was almost laughable in its transparency.

His amateur subterfuge might have been comical if it hadn't been so deeply painful.

For months after I asked for a divorce, Chad tried to hoover me back in with declarations of love, grand gestures and bouts of "transparency." He'd thrust his unlocked computer or phone into my hands as some form of self-imposed penance. During those times, I saw emails, social media exchanges and even messages accompanying the extravagant gifts he sent to her.

And, I saw the language he had used with his online fiancée. He called her his "wife," his "soulmate," his "meant to be."

They hadn't just been exchanging messages; they had been actively planning a wedding. Emails flew back and forth as they coordinated every detail: "Did you book the celebrant?" "Is your dress ready?" "Are the tickets from New Zealand to Fiji confirmed for the honeymoon?"

But their exchanges weren't just romantic fluff. Their correspondence was a soap opera of drama, arguments, reconciliations and declarations of love.

To my astonishment, Becky knew Chad was still married for at least the last several months of their affair. She was fully aware that she was planning a wedding with a man who was already someone else's husband.

In hindsight, I wonder if Becky, too, was caught in her own version of his web. We were both sold the same false promises.

One of the most surreal exchanges I saw between them revolved around a business trip Chad and I took to Paris in late 2021. By that point, I sensed trouble in our marriage, though I hadn't yet discovered the affair. Becky, however, expressed outrage that Chad had dared to travel to Paris with his own wife.

"Being here without you is unbearable," Chad wrote to her from the City of Light. *"I can't wait to hold you in my arms in just four short weeks and show you how much you mean to me."* (This was likely a reference to one of the many secret trips he had planned to New Zealand, despite COVID-19 border closures.)

Becky's response was explosive. She couldn't understand how a man supposedly devoted to her could travel overseas with his wife. *"A real man would say, 'No, my loyalty is with Becky. I'm about to leave my wife for her!' Was everything a lie? Just some fantasy?"*

True to form, Chad responded with theatrical assurances: *"True love doesn't disappear. I'm still the man you love … flawed but devoted to you."*

And so, their cycle of melodrama continued.

In hindsight, their relationship was a mirror image of the one I'd once had with Chad, minus the adultery and dramatics. The same grand promises, the same hollow declarations, the same meticulously crafted facade. I realized, with bitter clarity, that he was simply recycling his narcissistic playbook.

To Becky, Chad seemed to fashion himself as a Christian Gray type: a fantasy projection of dominance and allure that, like the rest of his persona, crumbled under scrutiny. He had painted himself as an accomplished American author writing under a pseudonym, a wealthy CEO commanding a team of executives and a powerful "alpha male."

The reality? He ran a modest social media page where most followers thought he was a woman, co-owned a struggling consulting firm barely turning a profit and drove a car that I had largely financed. The "alpha male" image? A flimsy cover for insecurity and shame.

In my understanding, their in-person romance — when it finally happened — unraveled in less than 24 hours. I can only speculate about what transpired during their brief encounter, but it's clear that neither of them lived up to the elaborate personas they had built for one another … and certainly not the stuff of true hopes and dreams.

Oh, to have been a fly on that wall.

From my vantage point now, years removed, I can see the absurdity of it all. Chad was a man trapped in a world of make-believe, tirelessly constructing personas, grand illusions and intricate lies. The most outlandish part? He seemed utterly convinced that no one could see through him.

Looking back, I've realized that his betrayal wasn't just about infidelity; it was about the elaborate life he fabricated and the countless ways he manipulated those around him. The pain of it was real, but so was the preposterousness.

Now, with time and distance, I can laugh, not only at the sheer ridiculousness of it all, but also at how far I've come since then.

Chapter 16: Lies, Fantasies & Heavily Edited Photos

In all of Chad and Becky's exchanges about the future that I saw – browsing apartments online, planning restaurants to try, mapping out trips to take, even discussing wedding venues and officiants – there was one glaring omission: Chad never once mentioned divorcing me.

What was his plan? I still don't fully know. Though the questions rumbled around in my brain incessantly … was he envisioning maintaining two marriages and two families on opposite sides of the world? Planning to slip away and serve me divorce papers from New Zealand? Or simply stringing Becky along, keeping the fantasy alive just enough to maintain her devotion?

He had already tried twice to reach New Zealand during COVID-19 border closures, carrying what appeared to be fabricated documents and what I assume were more lies than truths. I discovered these "papers" when they synced to the shared photo editing app we both used – a gut-punch moment that crystallized the sheer arrogance of believing he could outsmart an entire nation's government.

With that level of hubris and detachment from reality, I suppose the idea of carrying on two parallel lives didn't seem so far-fetched to him. For me, however, the entire scenario felt like something ripped from a Netflix drama, not my actual life.

But in a sea of fiction-worthy twists, perhaps the most mind-boggling was learning that Chad and Becky hadn't even had a virtual face-to-face conversation until shortly before their 18-month affair unraveled.

For nearly a year and a half, he spent hours each night locked in his car, supposedly "listening to music." In reality, he was on the phone with her. Yet, in all that time, not one FaceTime, Zoom or Skype call?

Most people in long-distance romances would make video chats a priority. But they apparently avoided it … until one day, they finally took the plunge. The email exchange that followed made it clear why they had waited so long.

"Did you find me that unattractive?" Becky wrote to him afterward, seeming uneasy after their call, just a couple of weeks before they planned to meet in person. *"Why the change in how you treat me after our first video chat?"*

"If there's any change, Becky, it's on your side," Chad replied. *"Maybe I didn't meet your expectations."*

"We all have bad days," she shot back defensively. *"I told you it was early, and I was just dehydrated, Chad. And a video doesn't tell the whole story. I know exactly what I look like."*

"Why do you keep bringing up looks?" he countered. *"Is there something you're trying to say?"*

The back-and-forth deflection and manipulation in their messages was staggering. "Who was catfishing whom?" I wondered. "How could this even be real?"

But one thing became glaringly obvious to me: their relationship seemed to be built on illusions, exaggerated promises and heavily edited photos.

As I pieced together the details of Chad's affair, I felt an unexpected mix of emotions. The familiar ache of betrayal was still there, of course, but alongside it was something new: relief. Each absurd revelation unraveled another strand of the web of manipulation that had held me captive.

At times, the ludicrousness of it all was almost laughable – like a soap opera brought to life. Almost.

I'd been here before, each time I uncovered Chad's flirtations with other women or his elaborate lies. Each new discovery forced me to confront how much of our relationship had been real and how much had been pure fabrication. And each time, the gut punch of betrayal returned.

But self-doubt continued to creep in, whispering insidious questions: "Could I have done more? Could I have tried harder?"

"No," I reminded myself. "This was never about me."

The more I learned, the more I saw how small Chad's world really was. He wasn't the man I'd once believed him to be. The man who had promised me the world had spent half of our "marriage" writing groveling love letters to someone he had never met, desperately clinging to a fantasy built on nothing but deception.

It might have been comical – if it hadn't been my reality.

Looking back, I can see how meticulously Chad seemed to craft his illusions. Whether it was with his body, his career or his relationships, he presented carefully curated personas. But over time, those facades began to show cracks, and the reality beneath them became impossible to ignore.

The affair wasn't just the breaking point; it was the moment of clarity I needed. For so long, I had clung to the hope of who Chad could be, the version of him I thought I'd married. But in the end, I realized he wasn't just lying to me, he was lying to himself. And that wasn't something I could fix.

"This," I thought, "is what I've been holding on to? A fantasy? A facade? A man too insecure to even face the truth with himself?"

When I finally came to these realizations, a strange calm settled over me. I no longer felt the need to fix things. I didn't need to cling to hope or make excuses for his behavior. I was done.

In the end, Chad and Becky seemed to be a perfect match: bound by their shared illusions, deception and the fantasy they had created together. And while Becky may never have realized it, her role in all of this gave me an unexpected gift – the final push I needed to break free.

Sometimes, truth really is stranger than fiction.

Chapter 17: Secret Plans

While Chad and I do not share children, we did share a business. In January 2022, just days after discovering irrefutable proof of his affair – displayed publicly on social media, complete with a second Facebook profile declaring himself engaged to Becky – I began working with my lawyers. My priorities were clear: protect my stake in the business, secure my assets and ensure my children's well-being as I prepared for the divorce. All of this, months before Chad even realized I was aware of his deceit.

While I meticulously worked with my legal team, Chad continued pursuing his own "secret plans." Later that month, I came across a one-way plane to New Zealand that he had booked for a date that spring. This ticket was the final piece of evidence I needed – undeniable proof of his ongoing affair and his intention to leave.

As mentioned earlier, this was at least the third plane ticket Chad had purchased to New Zealand. Yet, despite his determination, he had never actually set foot in the country. (You'd think being turned away at the airline check-in once during a pandemic would be enough … but if nothing else, Chad was persistent.)

By now, I was familiar with his patterns. As with his earlier failed attempts, I knew he wouldn't tell me about the trip until the last possible moment, likely framing it as a spontaneous decision born out of "depression" and his need for self-reflection.

"I'll come back whole and happy, and then we can be whole and happy," he would promise. "It will be like it was."

And I, playing my role, would cry real tears, pretending to believe him.

Behind the scenes, however, I worked tirelessly to finalize the paperwork formalizing my co-ownership of the business before his departure. Just one week before his flight, I presented him with the documents. Chad signed without hesitation, so confident in his web of lies that he failed to recognize the ground shifting beneath him.

With the business secure, I could finally shift my focus to the next phase: ending the marriage.

One of the hardest parts of this entire ordeal was the act I had to maintain. For months, I pretended to be oblivious: the devoted wife who suspected nothing. It was a role I despised, but one I knew was necessary. My attorney and I had devised a protective strategy that hinged on keeping my knowledge of Chad's affair secret.

I needed Chad to take that trip. Upon his return, I would ask for a divorce, citing irreconcilable differences. I planned to reference his erratic behavior, his spontaneous and extended absences, and our growing incompatibility. But one thing I would not mention? The affair.

If Chad contested the divorce or tried to lay claim to my assets, I was prepared to demand a forensic accounting of our finances. This would force him to reveal his separate accounts and credit card transactions, which I was confident would expose the affair and any financial misconduct related to our business. I counted on Chad's desperation to keep his double life hidden, trusting he would prioritize protecting his "secrets" over pursuing my assets.

When we entered the marriage, almost every asset – from retirement accounts to savings to the home we lived in – was mine. I was determined to leave the marriage the same way.

Some might call my approach cold and calculated. Calculated? Certainly. But cold? No. It was simply fair.

Why should a man who had already taken so much from me – emotionally, financially and professionally – walk away with even more? Why should I allow him to profit further from my years of hard work, savings and careful planning?

I wasn't asking for anything of his. Whatever funds Chad had left were likely overseas anyway, tucked away in the jewelry box of a woman he barely knew. I didn't care what he chose to do with his resources; I cared only about protecting my own.

In the end, safeguarding my children, my assets and my future wasn't just a necessity: it was a quiet but powerful victory in a battle I never should have had to fight.

Chapter 18: His Crisis,
My Emergency

Chad's third and final attempt to travel to New Zealand was the one that finally succeeded. It was during this trip that he met his online fiancée. His first two attempts, however, ended in failure, both thwarted at U.S. airports.

By the time Chad announced his first planned trip to New Zealand, he had already spent months in his car each evening, supposedly "listening to music." In reality, he was spending hours on the phone with Becky. I didn't know this at the time, but I knew something felt off.

It was spring 2021, and the world was just starting to reopen after the height of the COVID-19 pandemic. I had planned my first work trip in over a year, to a conference in Austin, and invited Chad to join me.

My mom had graciously agreed to stay with Aiden and Jacob while we traveled, and I hoped the trip might offer us a chance to reconnect. Chad agreed to come along, even letting me purchase his plane ticket. What I didn't know was that he had a very different itinerary in mind. Unbeknownst to me, he had secretly booked a flight to New Zealand for the same day as my trip to Austin. His plan? To carpool to the airport with me before heading off on his own international escapade. Thoughtful, right?

When Chad finally dropped this bombshell, just two days before our departure, I was floored.

"Wait, what?" I asked, trying to process his outlandish announcement. "You're leaving for six weeks … to go to New Zealand?"

"Yes," he replied flatly. "I told you I needed to take a trip, to have some time alone. I need to fix myself so I can come home and fix us."

"I thought you meant a week in a cabin somewhere in North Carolina," I said, struggling to wrap my head around the scale of his plans. "This is extreme!"

"What does it matter where I go?" he countered, slipping effortlessly into his usual gaslighting tactics. "I'll be gone either way."

"Because it's halfway around the world!" I exclaimed, hoping he'd realize how absurd this was.

"And?" His tone was cold, indifferent.

We went around in circles, with Chad dismissing every concern I raised with icy detachment. By the end, I was emotionally drained and out of words. Eventually, I gave up.

Two days later, we drove to the airport in my car. I carried a small suitcase packed for four days of a work conference. Chad, meanwhile, hauled two oversized bags, supposedly for six weeks of solitude and "introspection." In reality, I now believe he was gearing up for an extended romantic adventure with Becky.

At the airline counter, his grand plan began to unravel. The airline agent informed him that he could not board the plane without proper documentation: flying to New

Zealand with just a U.S. passport was not possible during the strict pandemic border closures.

And just like that, Chad's crisis became my emergency.

He claimed he couldn't return to the house, not with my mom there watching the boys. How could he face her after his dramatic announcement? Now, he insisted, he had no choice but to join me on my trip to Texas.

So right there in the airport terminal, I repurchased his ticket to Austin – the same one I had canceled just two days earlier. While I made the arrangements, Chad promised me that he would never spring another last-minute trip on me again.

That promise lasted only a few months. He broke it on December 22, just three days before Christmas.

Chapter 19: New Zealand Bound

The house was festive, the Christmas tree adorned with twinkling lights and stacked with presents for Chad, Aiden and Jacob. The stockings were hung, and I clung to hope. I had worked hard to create a warm, joyful atmosphere. Christmas has always been my favorite time of year, and I was determined that this year, we would have a perfect family holiday.

"Maybe I should have known better," I would later reflect.

As Christmas approached, Chad's mood darkened – a familiar pattern he used before dropping unexpected, self-serving decisions on me. On December 22, just three days before the holiday, he announced that he that had once again purchased a one-way ticket to New Zealand.

"One-way," he said, as if this showed flexibility. "So I can come back whenever it feels right."

"But not longer than six weeks," he added, as though this softened the blow.

This time, I wasn't shocked; I was furious. "Are you serious?" I snapped, my frustration sharp.

"Yes," Chad said flatly. "I'm just not feeling the Christmas spirit, so I can't be here for the holidays."

"You're not feeling the Christmas spirit?" I repeated, disbelief thick in my voice. "What about Aiden? What about Jacob? What about me? It's not all about you."

Chad, quick to dismiss my feelings, replied, "The boys won't care or remember anyway."

And just like that, on December 23, 2021, Chad left. His excuse about "needing to escape the holiday" concealed a darker truth – one I wouldn't fully uncover until later. As I would come to learn, this wasn't a spontaneous decision; Chad had purchased the ticket weeks earlier. He wasn't escaping Christmas; he was rushing toward Becky. He had even sent her a fake Christmas tree and elaborate gifts for their "special" celebration.

Saddened but not surprised, I watched him leave. No amount of rationalizing, excuses or explanations could make his decision to abandon his family on Christmas seem less selfish or less cruel.

But fate had other plans for Chad. Upon arriving in Los Angeles, having booked the legs of his trip separately, he was once again turned away at the gate. New Zealand's borders were still firmly closed due to COVID restrictions. Apparently, not even Chad's arrogance could outwit an entire nation's government.

Two days of flights, layovers and denials later, he walked back through the door. My mom, Aiden, Jacob and I were in the middle of what had become a peaceful and joyful Christmas Day – our first one in years. Chad looked exhausted, his face a mask of feigned repentance, already maneuvering to reclaim control of the narrative.

"I've learned my lesson," he declared dramatically. "I'm committed to making things right."

But I was no longer buying it.

His words, which might have inspired hope in me before, only cemented my growing resolve. I couldn't fix him. I couldn't save our marriage. And I couldn't keep sacrificing for someone who had already checked out.

Just days after his return, I uncovered undeniable evidence of his affair. Any lingering doubts I had evaporated in that moment. There was no gaslighting that could twist the facts. Chad's attempts to conceal his infidelity – and the fantasy life he'd been building with Becky – were unraveling before my eyes.

Quietly, I began working with my lawyer, laying the groundwork for a divorce that would protect my sons, my assets and my future.

By the time Chad booked his third and final trip to New Zealand (the moment their borders reopened later that year), I was prepared. I had known this moment was coming, and I was ready.

He left on a Sunday afternoon for a woman he had never met but to whom he had promised a future. True to form, he spun yet another flimsy story, claiming he had only decided to leave and booked the ticket that morning. It wasn't true, of course, but I didn't argue.

"Let him think he's clever," I thought. "His delusions work in my favor now."

Despite knowing the truth and having already set my plans in motion to end our marriage, I couldn't stop the wave of devastation that hit me when Chad walked out the door.

"He's gone. Please come," I texted my mom, sisters and closest friends.

And they came, arriving with snacks, wine and open arms. And I finally allowed myself to cry.

I cried for the years I had wasted. I cried for the lies, the betrayal and the false hope I had clung to for far too long.

But as the evening wore on, my tears began to change. Alongside the grief, I felt relief. The weight of it all – the manipulation, the gaslighting, the exhaustion – was starting to lift.

I wasn't just mourning what I had lost; I was making room for what was ahead. Though the wounds were fresh, an undeniable sense of strength was taking root.

This chapter was closing. And for the first time in years, I could see the outline of a better, brighter life waiting for me on the other side.

Chapter 20: What Hopes & Dreams Are Made Of

Chad said he'd be gone for about six weeks. I didn't know if it would be six weeks or forever. In the end, it was less than six days, including nearly 48 hours of travel.

He arrived in New Zealand on a Monday. By Thursday afternoon, he was texting me from a plane on his way back home. It seemed the "love of his life" wasn't what hopes and dreams were made of after all.

Chad claimed he was happy. He told me he had found clarity, learned everything he needed to about himself and his love for me. With grandiose promises, he vowed that once he returned, everything would finally be exactly as it should have been all along.

This time, though, I saw through it. His declarations felt hollow. His promises no longer carried weight. I had already decided: I was done.

After more than 24 hours of travel, Chad arrived home on a Friday evening. When I didn't greet him with the joy he clearly expected, he turned cold.

"Things will get ugly if your attitude doesn't change," he declared.

It was staggering – even then, after everything, he remained confident in the control he thought he still had over me. His tone wasn't one of repentance but rather of someone accustomed to wielding power through intimidation. What he failed to realize was that his power was gone.

The next morning, just 12 hours after his return, I told him I wanted a divorce.

Chad was stunned. He wept. He wailed. He pounded his fists on the furniture. He begged. He professed his love and promised change. Yet amidst all of his dramatics, I felt something unexpected: calm.

That's not to say there wasn't grief. I still suffered, still mourned the loss of the man and marriage I thought I had. But even in my pain, I was healing. I was reclaiming myself. My strength. My confidence. My life.

The divorce process itself moved quickly. The morning after Chad returned, I presented the papers, asking for his signature each week for two months until he finally complied. He signed the paperwork in May, and the divorce was finalized just 30 days later.

During those two months, Chad oscillated between stalling and love bombing, delaying the inevitable while attempting to pull me back into his orbit. But I remained resolute.

The steps were clear: protect the business (check), secure my assets (check), draft the divorce papers (check), deliver the request (check), finalize the process (check). The to-do list was straightforward. But the emotional toll was anything but.

For months, I had had to keep my knowledge of the affair and my plans for divorce hidden from Chad. I pretended everything was fine. I waved him off with a smile as he left to "listen to music," fully aware that he would be spending that time on the phone with Becky. I stayed silent when I stumbled upon the engagement ring meant for her. I ignored the blatant lies about his "spontaneous" trips to New Zealand. I bit my tongue when all I wanted to do was scream, demand answers and confront him with the reality of what he had done.

I stayed silent because I had to, knowing that his "secret" was my most powerful leverage.

But I wasn't perfect. Cracks appeared in my composure at times, moments when my resolve slipped, and I couldn't help but push just a little.

One evening, in a flash of frustration and wry defiance, I texted Chad a series of heavily edited photos of myself.

"Can you believe what filters can do? Wild!" I wrote, as though I were simply playing around with the editing tools everyone uses on social media.

Then, I waited. I pictured him comparing the photos to her public images on Facebook – pictures that, to my eye, also seemed suspiciously polished and enhanced. I imagined his fingers flying across his phone screen, zooming in, spinning himself into a quiet tailspin as he crafted accusatory or defensive messages. For a moment, it gave me the tiniest bit of catharsis.

Another evening, my patience wore even thinner. I waited until he had retreated to the driveway for one of his nightly "music" sessions and then followed him outside. I opened the passenger-side door abruptly, startling him. He scrambled to end the call I knew he would be on, but not before I caught a glimpse of Becky's photo illuminated on the dashboard's call display.

"I thought you were listening to music," I said, my voice deceptively light.

"I was," Chad stammered, barely missing a beat, "but I had to call Anthony." He named one of our male clients without hesitation.

"Oh, okay," I said, pretending to accept his answer. I asked the trivial question I had prepared as my pretext for interrupting, then walked back inside.

Later that night, Chad attempted damage control, handing me his phone with an air of exaggerated nonchalance. He pointed out a manipulated call log in which Becky's number had been deleted, replaced by a hasty call to Anthony. It was a clumsy, transparent attempt to reinforce his lie.

But no amount of manipulation could convince me anymore. I saw it all for what it was.

Though only a few months passed between discovering the affair and finalizing the divorce, those months felt endless. Even after I asked for a divorce, Chad refused to leave my house until the paperwork was finalized and he had no choice but to move out.

Living under the same roof as Chad during those weeks was one of the hardest things I've ever endured. He reverted to a full-on campaign of affection, acting as though we could rebuild what had already crumbled beyond repair. It was a performance – the role of the doting husband – and I had a front-row seat to the show every day. Meanwhile, I was working to untangle myself from the trauma bond that had kept me tethered for so long.

As someone who values honesty, living within a reality shaped by deception was unbearable. I felt trapped in a narrative constructed by someone for whom lies had become second nature. At the same time, I was confronting painful truths, all while enduring the love bombing of a man I no longer recognized who was wearing the face of someone I had once loved.

What saved me during those excruciating months was my support network. My friends and family stood beside me, steadfast and unwavering. They reminded me of my worth, my strength and the person I had always been – even when I struggled to see her. Their love and encouragement became my lifeline, tethering me to reality when I felt untethered and helping me remember that I was capable, I was enough, and I was never truly alone.

This was not the ending I had envisioned when I said, "I do." But by the time the divorce was finalized, I no longer mourned the life I once thought I had. Instead, I was looking forward to the life I was finally free to build.

Chapter 21: Complaints & Diatribes

Chad seemed to understand the power of a support network, perhaps even more than I realized at the time. My connection with my family had always been a source of strength, a foundation that could help me weather any storm. But over time, I noticed subtle shifts: moments where Chad appeared to undermine those ties, driving a wedge between me and the people who loved me most.

My family is generous, welcoming and kind. When Chad and I first got together, and I seemed happy, they greeted him with open arms. They tried to engage him, to make him feel included.

But from the beginning, Chad kept his distance. At family events, he rarely greeted anyone, often retreating to a corner with his head buried in his phone.

"I'm just not good at hellos and goodbyes," he'd say dismissively, as though that excused his behavior.

Conversations with Chad weren't easy either. He approached interactions like debates, as though every exchange was an opportunity to prove himself right or smarter than everyone else.

Early on, my sisters began to pull back, finding him argumentative and off-putting. My brothers-in-law were more reserved, but later, they shared their own stories of passive-aggressive remarks that left them feeling dismissed or insulted. But these confessions came only after my marriage to Chad was over.

Looking back, I see how Chad's behavior created distance between my family and me. One early example was when he asked my mom and sisters to help plan a surprise party for my 40th birthday. They poured their hearts into it, handling all the logistics and details. But on the day of the party, Chad soaked up the praise, basking in the spotlight as if the entire event had been his doing.

At gatherings, he would pick trivial arguments, tell unnecessary lies or push buttons just to get a rise out of others. Then, he'd withdraw, leaving others to deal with the aftermath of the conflict he had instigated.

The real damage, however, wasn't done in public. Behind closed doors, Chad's words planted seeds of doubt in me about my own family.

"They don't treat you the way you deserve," he'd say. "They undervalue you. They exclude you. You've always been the outsider, and they like it that way."

When I defended my family, he would brush me off, suggesting I was too naïve to see the slights he insisted were there. He knew how to zero in on insecurities I had shared with him, amplifying my doubts and fears until they felt overwhelming.

Chad also struggled to celebrate others' successes, especially those of my family. When someone achieved something meaningful, he often diminished their accomplishments, questioning their worth or integrity. Over time, his negativity wore me down. It became easier to limit interactions with my family rather than endure Chad's endless complaints and diatribes afterward.

At the heart of it all, Chad seemed deeply uncomfortable or unhappy when anyone else became the center of attention. If I dared to shine, or if my focus shifted away from him, his resentment flared.

One moment that still stands out happened a few months into our relationship, at my cousin's wedding in Connecticut. It was a perfect day: the bride was radiant, the groom charming and the reception filled with love, laughter and celebration. Seated with my sisters, brothers-in-law and cousins, I was in my element, enjoying the easy flow of conversation and the happiness of being surrounded by my family.

But as the night wore on, Chad grew more withdrawn. While everyone else danced and reveled in the joy of the evening, I saw him sitting alone on the steps of the venue across the lawn, staring at his phone.

Then came the texts.

"You're ignoring me," he wrote. "You're selfish and cold."

"I'm leaving," came another message. "I would never treat you this way."

I was confused and heartbroken. "Treated you what way?" I texted back. "We're all having a great time."

Feeling like I had done something wrong, I left the reception earlier than I wanted, abandoning the laughter and bonding I was enjoying with my family to soothe Chad's wounded pride.

Later, I realized the real mistake wasn't anything I did that night. My only error was bringing Chad to the wedding at all.

This behavior became a pattern at family gatherings. If I was happy, engaged or focused on anyone else, Chad found a way to disrupt it. The worst incident came at my sister's 30th birthday party (detailed in *Chapter 28: Your Village*), but the result was always the same: I spent less time with my family and more time isolated, trapped in the toxic bubble Chad had worked to create.

Chapter 22: Mourning the Death of a Man Who Never Existed

Despite Chad's efforts to isolate me, my family and friends rallied around me when I needed them most. They offered unwavering love, strength and support, lifting me up in ways I never knew were possible.

I'll forever be grateful to my friends, my sisters and my mom for holding me together while I was shattering under the weight of grief and stress.

The months between uncovering Chad's affair and finalizing the divorce were some of the darkest of my life. I couldn't eat, I started anxiety medication for the first and only time, and I regularly struggled to catch my breath. At times, it felt as though my body was failing me, buckling under the emotional strain.

And yet, I wasn't alone. My family and friends became my lifelines. They dropped everything to support me in my moments of need: taking my calls at all hours, speaking soothing words while I cried and sitting with me through moments when it felt impossible to move forward.

Because Chad and I both worked from home, I couldn't make these calls inside the house. Instead, I would quietly step outside, find the nearest curb beyond the view of the windows and call one of my sisters.

"I can't breathe," I gasped one afternoon, my voice trembling. Without hesitation, my sister stayed with me on the phone, her own busy day falling to the wayside as she talked me through the moment. Her words held me steady while I felt like I was crumbling.

These moments repeated countless times with my mom, my sisters and my closest friends. They were patient, kind and steadfast. Their love reminded me of who I was when I couldn't see it for myself.

My mom described it best: I wasn't just mourning the end of my marriage; I was mourning the death of a man who had never truly existed. The Chad I thought I loved was a carefully constructed facade – a love-bombing mask he wore to win me over. And now, that mask had been ripped away, exposing truths I couldn't ignore.

Even though I knew intellectually that the person I was grieving had never been real, the pain of that loss was no less profound. My emotions were raw, overwhelming and impossible to ignore.

Experts often recommend going no-contact after a toxic relationship; I agree, it's sound advice. No-contact is one of the strongest tools for breaking free from the fog of a trauma bond. But for me, it wasn't an option. Chad and I shared a business, one I had built from the ground up, and I wasn't willing to walk away from it.

Thus, I had to find a way to break the trauma bond while still maintaining communication with the person who had created it.

As if that weren't enough, it often felt as though Chad was trying to hoover me back in. He leaned into old tactics, putting the mask back on and love-bombing me with grand promises in what seemed like an attempt to make me believe he could be the man I had once thought he was.

In those moments, I turned to my support network.

"Give me the hard truths," I would text them when I felt myself weakening and the fog of doubt began to creep in.

Staying – indulging in the magical thinking that things could somehow be different – might have seemed easier in the short term. But I knew that path too well. It would lead back to the same cycle of lies and heartbreak, pulling me even deeper into the haze I was fighting to escape.

So, I leaned on my friends and family, asking them to ground me when I couldn't trust my own perceptions, asking them for the hard truths.

And they would tell me my own stories, stories I had lived but needed to hear again. They reminded me of the lies I had uncovered, the pain I had endured and the patterns I could no longer unsee. They recounted the moments they had witnessed of Chad's manipulation and deceit, of the lies and abuses toward my children and myself. They held up a mirror, revealing the truths of my past and present to help me see through the fog.

With love and with patience, they helped me break my own heart again and again until, finally, he was gone, and I could heal.

Chapter 23: Prelude to Part 3 – Turning the Page

The chapters you've just read were some of the hardest to write. Revisiting the pain, betrayal and layers of manipulation wasn't easy. But I didn't share those moments to dwell in the darkness – I shared them because they're a part of the story, and more importantly, a part of the transformation. They shaped me, but they don't define me. And your darkest times don't have to define you either.

If you've made it this far, I imagine you've faced your own version of heartbreak, loss or uncertainty. Maybe you've carried the weight of a relationship that took more than it gave. Or perhaps you're at a crossroads, staring at a life that feels unrecognizable, wondering how to take that first step forward.

Let me tell you, as someone who has been there: you are not broken, you are not stuck, and you are not alone.

Part 3 is where we shift focus: from surviving to creating the lives we truly want to live. It's no longer just about my journey; it's about yours too. Together, we'll take what may feel fractured, lost or overwhelming and transform it into something strong, resilient and uniquely, beautifully yours.

This is where we move from mourning what was to building what can be.

In the chapters ahead, I'll share tools, strategies and lessons that helped me rebuild my life – not as a patched-up version of what it used to be, but as something brighter, fuller and more authentic than I ever imagined. These insights are woven together with stories and experiences that I hope will inspire and guide you.

These aren't quick fixes or one-size-fits-all solutions. They're choices, mindsets and practices that helped me reclaim my power, rediscover joy and chart a life that feels deeply true to me.

Now it's your turn. It's time to turn the page and begin writing the next chapter of your story.

Let's do this – together.

Part 3:
A Shared Journey
TURNING SURVIVING INTO THRIVING

Chapter 24: The Hard Truths

We have all suffered. Some of us are suffering now. If you've already left or repaired a challenging situation, I'm so happy for you. If you've never faced a troubled relationship, I'm even happier for you.

But if you're still in one, and you don't want to be, I implore you to seek the help and support you may need. You don't have to face it alone. Reading this book is a great start, but it's only the beginning. I encourage you to reach out: find a counselor, lean on trusted confidants and advisors, and let your circle help you.

Asking for help has never been my strength; it's something I've always struggled with. For a long time, I thought I had to carry my burdens alone, that no one could or would understand. But here's what I've learned: people who love you want to help. They want to be there for you. You just have to let them in.

When I was struggling the most, each person I allowed into my world became a lifeline. With every conversation, every moment of connection, I grew a little stronger. Through their patient and loving eyes, words and arms, I started to see myself again. They didn't just listen; they encouraged me, supported me and reminded me of my worth. And when I asked, they told me the hard truths I needed to hear.

The few weeks between asking for a divorce and Chad finally moving out were some of the most challenging and transformative of my life. His love bombing was in overdrive, and while we were in separate bedrooms, we were still living under the same roof, watching TV in the same living room, eating at the same table.

He tried everything to hoover me back in, playing the part of the perfect husband, suddenly eager to repent and repair.

"Let's go to couples counseling," he'd say. "Some of the strongest marriages are ones that overcame infidelity. This could be the best thing that ever happens for our relationship."

"I didn't love her. I was never planning to leave," he insisted. "I was just bored. I know now how wrong it was."

"I was just using her to gain entry into New Zealand," he claimed. "You know how important it was for me to go there to find myself."

"It wasn't even real," he said. "It was a game."

Though I recognized the manipulation, the gaslighting and the lies in every promise he made, a small voice in the back of my mind – the lingering remnant of the trauma bond – would still whisper, "What if he could change? What if I'm wrong?"

In those moments, it would have been easier for me to believe him. And a small part of my exhausted heart wanted to.

It would have been simpler to stop fighting, to stop doing the hard work to free myself of that man and that marriage. It would have been easier to give in to his words, to pretend everything would magically be okay. To convince myself that happiness was still possible if we could just go back to the illusion of those early days.

But deep down, I knew better. I knew that anything he was promising was a lie: a temporary fix at best. If I stayed, I'd eventually find myself right back where I started, only worse: weaker and more broken.

Still, I couldn't entirely trust my own judgment. My perspective was clouded by the trauma bond I was working to break. Even as clarity slowly emerged, I knew my lens was still distorted, fogged by years of gaslighting and manipulation.

So, I turned to my mom, my sisters and my friends – the people I trusted most.

"Tell me the hard truths," I would say.

And they would. Until I could trust myself, I trusted them instead.

The Hard Truths

My story might sound familiar to you, or it might not. But what's important is this: every relationship that drains your strength and clouds your vision – whether romantic or platonic, professional or personal – deserves to be examined with honesty.

If you feel immured in a storm of uncertainty, I encourage you to ask your trusted family and friends for their thoughts and perspectives. Maybe what you're feeling and seeing is accurate, or maybe, like me, you need trusted voices to help you see what you can't. Your loved ones may offer insights that help you determine whether it's worth staying and working to improve the relationship or if leaving is the best path forward.

I can't assess your situation. But I do know this: whatever decision you make will be the right one if it's made with a clear mind, a focused heart and a sense of optimism for the future.

That said, if you aren't ready to ask your circle just yet but need a place to start, here are the hard truths I uncovered along the way.

And, when you're ready, add your own.

Hard Truths from My Journey

On the Reality of the Relationship
The Chad I loved never existed. He was a facade, a front designed to manipulate me.

The future I imagined with Trip was an illusion propped up by magical thinking. I couldn't cure his struggles, and nothing would change until he chose to seek help.

Just because they didn't hit me didn't mean it wasn't abuse. Abuse comes in many forms: emotional, psychological, verbal – all of it damaging.

Narcissistic abuse is toxic and very real. The cycle may be difficult to break, but it is worth it.

On Self-Worth and Empowerment
I was enough. I always was. I didn't need to change myself for someone else's love or approval.

I was worthy. My value was never in question, no matter what they made me believe.

My children and I deserved so much better. We didn't have to settle for toxic love. We were worthy of peace, joy and healthy love.

On the Power of Letting Go
My dreams were mine to achieve. They weren't tied to Chad or that relationship.

I was better off alone than with an abusive or narcissistic partner. Choosing yourself and your peace is the first step to reclaiming your life.

On Forgiving Myself

To echo Al-Anon's Three Cs: I didn't cause Trip's struggles, I couldn't control them, and I certainly couldn't cure them. No amount of love or patience could fix him – only he had the power to do that.

It was ok to "not let things go" when they were still unresolved. My feelings were valid, and I deserved resolution, not dismissal.

On Trusting the Process and Yourself

Prioritizing my well-being wasn't selfish. I deserved happiness, too.

I wasn't being too sensitive. Gaslighting made me question my reactions, but my feelings were valid. My instincts were guiding me toward the truth.

I was strong and capable. Even when I doubted myself, I had the strength and resilience to overcome the pain and build something better.

On Moving Forward, Onward and Upward

I was worthy of more. I didn't have to settle for broken love. I was worthy of real, reciprocal affection.

Leaving was not a failure. Walking away from what no longer served me was a victory, not a defeat.

I could create a better future for myself and my children. By letting go of toxic relationships, I opened the door to a life filled with peace, joy and opportunity.

Your truths may look different from mine, but they are just as important.

Exercise: Listing Your Truths

Now that you've read through my hard truths, let's explore yours. This exercise is designed to help you gain clarity, build confidence and define what truly matters.

1. **Reflect and Highlight:** Revisit my truths and highlight the ones that resonate most.
2. **Write Your Own:** On the next page, write your personal truths – about your relationship, your self-worth and your path forward.
3. **Reflect on Their Importance:** Use space provided to journal about why these truths matter to you and how they can guide your decisions.

Final Thoughts

Until you can fully trust your own hard truths, let mine guide you. Use them as steppingstones to clarity and strength. Over time, your own truths will become clearer, stronger and uniquely yours.

And always remember: you are worthy. Your feelings are valid. Your needs matter. And you are important.

No one deserves to be criticized, blamed or punished. No one should endure gaslighting or manipulation. You don't have to stay in a destructive cycle or ride a rollercoaster of constant dramatics. That's not healthy. That's not a relationship. That is abuse.

You deserve to be protected, cherished, honored and loved. You deserve the future you dream of. And you are strong and capable enough to create it!

Your Hard Truths

_____

_____

_____

_____

_____

_____

_____

_____

_____

_____

_____

_____

_____

_____

_____

_____

_____

_____

_____

_____

Reflections

_____

_____

_____

_____

_____

_____

_____

_____

_____

_____

_____

_____

_____

_____

_____

Mantras for Strength, Peace and Clarity

During my turbulent relationships, I relied on mantras to ground myself, find peace and build strength. These simple yet powerful phrases became anchors in moments of doubt, tools for reflection and reminders of the resilience I carried within me.

Now, I'm sharing them with you.

Exercise: Reflect and Empower

On the following pages, highlight any mantras that resonate with you, add your own and revisit them whenever you need strength, inspiration or clarity.

Breaking a Trauma Bond

- I am courageous and strong enough to break free.
- I am worthy of love, respect and kindness.
- My past does not define me.
- I will set boundaries to protect my well-being.
- I trust myself to make the best decisions for my life.
- I am capable of healing and moving forward.
- I deserve happiness and will prioritize it.
- I am strong, resilient and capable.
- My worth is not tied to someone else's approval.
- My feelings are valid, and I am free to express them in healthy ways.
- I will not accept toxic relationships or manipulation.
- I trust I can find love, happiness, and fulfillment beyond this situation.

Breaking free takes courage, time and strength, but it's possible – and you are capable. Keep going. You're stronger than you know. And peace is waiting on the other side.

Breaking Free
Words to Live By

_____

_____

_____

_____

_____

_____

_____

_____

_____

_____

_____

_____

_____

Finding Clarity

- I let go of the noise of others' opinions and trust my own truths.
- My wisdom and intuition are my strongest guides.
- Every experience I encounter is a steppingstone toward greater clarity.
- I choose to focus my thoughts on positivity and understanding.
- I release distractions and find strength in stillness.
- I welcome the unknown as part of my journey to discovery.
- I am patient with myself as I gain insight and understanding.
- My past does not define me; my actions today shape my future.
- I seek truth in all aspects of my life.
- I trust myself and my inner voice.
- I know my worth and honor it every day.
- I am always evolving, growing and gaining wisdom.
- I let go of confusion and embrace peace and understanding.
- I find balance in uncertainty and trust that clarity will come.
- I am centered, focused and clear in my intentions.
- I am a source of clarity and calm in a chaotic world.

Seek clarity. Trust yourself. Trust the process.

Finding Clarity

Words to Live By

_____

_____

_____

_____

_____

_____

_____

_____

_____

_____

_____

_____

_____

_____

_____

_____

_____

Prioritizing Peace & Joy

- I de-escalate conflict within myself and choose peace over worry.
- Difficult situations refine me; they do not define me.
- I find joy in the journey, even when the road is rocky.
- I am a beacon of calm amidst the storms of life.
- I am resilient and ready to face any hardship.
- My spirit remains unbroken, no matter the difficulties I encounter.
- Every challenge brings an opportunity for me to grow and shine brighter.
- I find strength in my calm amidst the chaos.
- I am at peace, even when life is not perfect.
- I am greater than any challenge I face.
- I find joy in overcoming obstacles and moving forward.
- In the midst of difficulty, I am anchored in peace and buoyed by joy.
- My inner peace radiates outward, bringing light to my life.
- I am a master of my mind, not a slave to my circumstances.
- This too shall pass.

Set boundaries and anchor yourself in peace.

Final Thoughts

These mantras are more than just words: they are declarations of your strength, reminders of your worth and tools to help you navigate difficult moments. Keep them close. Speak them aloud. Return to them often.

Let them guide you toward the peace, clarity and empowerment you deserve.

Prioritizing Peace & Joy

Words to Live By

Chapter 25: The Courage to Heal

Healing is not linear. Even when a relationship, job or situation ends for all of the right reasons, loss and pain often follow ... the loss of the person, the dream or the future you once envisioned.

It's natural to mourn. Are you better off? Yes. Was it the right decision? Without a doubt. Should you ever go back? No. Are you still grieving? Of course.

And that's okay.

Experts talk about the five stages of grief: denial, anger, bargaining, depression and finally acceptance. But they are not linear. There is no perfect roadmap to healing, no guaranteed way to move from grief to acceptance and then to blissful indifference. There is no "right" way to grieve. You may find yourself revisiting anger or circling back to sadness, even when you thought you'd moved past those feelings. That's part of the process, and it's normal.

Allow yourself to feel your emotions. You have to *go* through them to *get* through them and ultimately to *grow* through them.

As you navigate this process, be gentle with yourself, give yourself grace. Lean on your support system, reflect on your journey, and, when you're ready, look toward the future. Onward and upward.

With Trip and the decision to stay in the marriage to protect my child, healing was gradual. Years before I physically left, I had already begun to emotionally detach. By the time I asked for a divorce, much of my healing had quietly taken place.

With Chad, it was different. The end felt sudden and jarring, and my healing and heartbreak unfolded simultaneously.

When I look back now, I can see the slow unraveling of my relationship with Chad: the indiscretions both small and large and the inexcusable behaviors that eroded the foundation long before it collapsed. But because the water had been heating up so gradually, and because the final catalyst – his online "fiancée" – was so shocking, the heartbreak and betrayal hit me all at once.

At the same time, as I began clearing the fog of his gaslighting, I started to see how problematic things had been all along. I had already been standing up for my children; now, for the first time, I was ready to stand up for myself.

At the beginning of the end, my emotions were 90% heartbreak and 10% healing. Over the subsequent months, those percentages shifted until finally I reached the golden light of indifference – a place where I could see that "marriage" for what it truly was.

When I confirmed Chad's affair, it was devastating, but it also came with a strange sense of relief. It confirmed that I wasn't "crazy" or "too sensitive." My instincts had been right all along. My heart was broken, but for the first time in a long while, I felt like I could trust myself again.

Once my eyes were opened to his ongoing infidelity, the clues he'd so casually toss around – assuming I was completely in the dark – became glaringly obvious. For example, he began buying cookies (or biscuits) that were popular in New Zealand and would "playfully" speak in his version of a New Zealand accent while eating them.

Each instance was both a gut punch and a severed tie – a painful but necessary release. It was a bittersweet dichotomy: every realization hurt, yet each one helped loosen the grip of the trauma bond that had held me captive.

And thus, I hurt, and I healed.

"I'm moving to New Zealand," he told a Facebook friend (yet another woman he had never met in real life but seemed to regularly use to validate his ego). *"Rya is sweet, but an alpha needs an alpha."*

At the time, reading that stung. But now, it's a memory that makes me laugh. In the end, my strength carried me through. These instances and examples became fuel to my fire, and how brightly I burned!

"You're the love of my life," he wrote to Becky. *"I don't know how to live without you."*

Those words, which once felt sacred, were suddenly hollow. Seeing them written to someone else was another painful but freeing reminder of just how false his promises had been.

Then there were the grand gestures: extravagant bouquets of flowers, boxes of jewelry and endless notes professing his devotion to Becky – all before they'd even met in person. Each one hurt, but each one also became part of the fire that burned away the lies and left me stronger.

"For my stunning wife … I hope these brighten your Friday," one message read.

"For one of the countless reasons I cherish you, need you, adore you, and will one day marry you."

"A Very Happy Birthday to My Love Becky … our last one spent apart. Love, Your husband, Chad."

"My beautiful wife, my world, my everything, my beautiful Becky. I can't wait to be in your arms.
Yours always,
Chad"

"Never forget how much you mean to me. I can't wait to come home to you and bring the next bouquet to you in person.
With all my love, Chad
p.s. Will you marry me?"

As painful as each message was, with every line I read – of which these are just a sampling – my inner fire grew brighter. Every word hurt, but every word also helped.

With each line, I felt myself growing stronger until, like a phoenix rising from the ashes, I was ready to emerge, renewed and restored.

So please know this: you are not alone. If you are hurting, take heart – healing is possible. You have reserves of strength you may not even realize are there, but when you are ready, they will carry you through.

You will survive, and then you will thrive. You will reach the other side, and happiness awaits you there.

Exercise: Reflecting on Your Healing Process

Every healing journey is deeply personal and unique. There is no right or wrong way to heal: only what works for you.

In my experience, journaling became a powerful tool to help me process my emotions. At times, it was simply a way to release anger; other times, it helped me dig deeper and do the inner work required to move forward.

Take some time to reflect on your journey. This exercise isn't about finding all the answers right away. It's about giving yourself the space to sort through your emotions, reflect on your challenges and acknowledge your growth.

And when you're ready, turn the page for mantras designed to support you as you continue your journey toward healing a broken heart.

Reflections

Mantras for Healing a Broken Heart

Healing from heartbreak takes time, but you possess the strength and resilience to overcome it. Use these mantras to guide you in your journey toward healing and self-love.

Remember: Highlight any mantras that resonate, add your own and return to this list whenever you need support.

- I am worthy of love and happiness.
- This pain won't last forever; I am healing every day.
- I am stronger than any heartbreak.
- I forgive myself and release all past hurt.
- My heart is open to healing, peace and new love.
- Healing takes time, and I'm patient with myself.
- I am my own source of love and joy.
- I release the past and embrace the present.
- I trust in my ability to find love again.
- I allow myself to feel fully and heal completely.
- I am defined by my resilience, not this heartbreak.
- Everything happens for a reason, and I trust the journey.
- I am surrounded by love, support and positivity.
- I deserve a healthy relationship built on mutual respect and joy.
- My worth is infinite and unwavering.
- I am whole and complete on my own.
- I let go of what no longer serves me.
- My happiness is my own creation.
- My most important relationship is with myself.

Healing takes time, but you are strong and resilient. Trust in yourself and know that you are not alone in this journey.

Healing Journey
Words to Live By

Chapter 26: Optimism in Action: Beyond Magical Thinking

"Love is better than anger. Hope is better than fear. Optimism is better than despair. So let us be loving, hopeful and optimistic. And we'll change the world."
— Jack Layton

Do you consider yourself to be an optimist?

Optimism is a powerful force, but it doesn't happen by accident. For some, it comes naturally, but for others, it's a skill – one that can be learned, practiced and nurtured. And the beauty of optimism is that it inspires action: when we believe things can improve, we're motivated to make them better.

As Jack Layton said, "Hope is better than fear. Optimism is better than despair. So let us be loving, hopeful and optimistic. And we'll change the world."

But optimism isn't about wishful thinking or blind faith. It's about combining hope with effort and taking purposeful steps to create the life you want.

So, how do you start fostering optimism in your life?

Focusing on What You Can Control

For me, relentless optimism begins with focusing on what I can control instead of dwelling on what I can't. It's about choosing my responses, directing my energy and putting my focus where it can make a difference. This mindset shifts me from feeling powerless to powerful — a critical distinction, especially during challenging times.

You can't control someone else's actions, for instance, but you can control your own reactions. Easier said than done, I know, but once you begin practicing this, it becomes one of your most powerful tools.

Take Trip, for example. He had a habit of picking fights. Early on, I often took the bait and would berate myself afterward for engaging, especially when the kids were around. Over time, I realized that while I couldn't change his behavior, I could change mine. I made a commitment to remove myself and my kids from the situation — whether it was leaving the room or even the house — instead of engaging in unproductive conflict.

That commitment led to a mantra I still rely on today: "Does this serve my bigger-picture goal or purpose? Does this support my endgame?"

This simple question helps me navigate everything from work challenges to personal relationships. It's not about avoiding conflict but about choosing your battles wisely.

For example, when Chad would lash out during the final years of running our business together, it would have been satisfying — and temporarily cathartic — to engage or retaliate. But I would stop and think, "Would it feel good to push his buttons right now?"

Absolutely.

"But does that serve my bigger-picture goal of maintaining peace or securing necessary paperwork?"

Not at all.

While sinking to his level might have been momentarily satisfying, I knew it wouldn't help me achieve my ultimate goals. Instead, I chose to remain professional, focused and composed, refusing to let his behavior dictate mine.

This doesn't mean rolling over and taking whatever anyone dishes out: it means playing chess while they play checkers. Sometimes, giving up a battle is how you win the war.

Practicing Gratitude

Gratitude is one of the most effective actions you can take to cultivate optimism. It shifts your perspective from what's missing to what's present.

But gratitude doesn't mean complacency. You can appreciate your blessings while still striving for more. For example, I'm deeply grateful for my career, but I continue to pursue new dreams and ventures. Gratitude and ambition can coexist beautifully.

Each day, take a moment to reflect on what you're thankful for: the people, opportunities or even small joys in your life. Write them down if it helps. Gratitude, like optimism, grows when practiced regularly.

Building a Circle of Optimism

Optimism thrives in good company. Just as you build a network of trusted advisors for guidance, you can create a circle of positivity. Surround yourself with people who inspire and uplift you. Just as negativity can drag you down, positivity can pull you up and push you forward. And optimism is contagious … when shared, it grows exponentially.

They say nothing influences your life's trajectory more than the people around you. Choose wisely.

Developing Resilience

Resilience – the ability to recover, adapt and keep going despite setbacks – is optimism in action. Think of it like a muscle: the more you work it, the stronger it becomes.

My experience with infertility tested my resilience in profound ways. Every month brought hope followed by disappointment. And every month forced a decision: to either recover and keep going or to let go.

That said, letting go isn't failure; sometimes, it's the strongest choice you can make. Had my last round of IVF failed, I would have done just that. Knowing when to release a dream requires as much courage and determination as chasing it.

Whether you persist or pivot, resilience is about finding the strength to keep moving forward – even if that means building a new dream.

Resilience isn't just about pushing forward; it's also about making peace with change.

Relying on Touchpoints

When I'm feeling low or struggling, I turn to tools that help me reset and refocus. I read uplifting mantras and listen to music that makes me feel unstoppable. I remind myself that, no matter the challenge I'm facing, this too shall pass, and things will get better, especially if I actively endeavor to make it so.

I am a firm believer in karma, luck and pixie dust – but I also believe in hard work. It's amazing how often effort creates opportunity.

Optimism vs. Magical Thinking

So how is optimism different from magical thinking?

Magical thinking is believing in unrealistic outcomes without effort. It's a narrative built on wishes rather than facts. It's hoping for change without taking the steps to make it happen.

For example, I once believed that my future with Trip would be happy and healthy "in five years." I pictured a life where his alcoholism would be magically cured, his anger would fade, and we would finally live happily ever after.

But that dream ignored reality: he wasn't willing to change, and nothing would improve unless he did. It was as if I expected a Fairy Godmother to descend from the heavens, wave her magic wand and make everything better.

Magical thinking relies on fantasies instead of facts.

Optimism, on the other hand, is grounded in reality. It's a hopeful outlook that embraces effort and persistence. It's about believing that, while challenges exist, you have the power to overcome them.

Optimism doesn't deny hard work — it embraces it.

The Bottom Line

If there's one thing I hope you take from this book, it's the importance of relentless optimism in action. Life will bring hardships, but you have the strength to overcome them.

Let go of magical thinking and the disappointment it breeds. Embrace and foster optimism, and you'll find that good things await you on the other side.

Anchoring Optimism in Gratitude

Optimism is not just a mindset: it's a practice. Gratitude is one of the cornerstones of this practice, helping to shift your perspective by focusing on what you have instead of what you lack.

Developing a habit of gratitude builds and strengthens optimism over time, training your mind to find positives even in challenging moments.

Exercise: Daily Gratitude Practice
Each day, take a few minutes to reflect and jot down:
1. What inspired you.
2. Things you're grateful for.
3. Moments that made you smile.
4. Something you're proud of.
5. And what you're looking forward to.

These reflections can be simple or profound. The goal is to root your mindset in hope and possibility. By focusing on the positives, you train yourself to see them more clearly, even when life feels hard.

Optimism grows with gratitude. Start small, and let the practice carry you forward.

Daily Gratitude Practice

DATE: _____

WHAT INSPIRED ME TODAY?

_____

_____

_____

_____

A MOMENT THAT MADE ME SMILE:	SOMETHING I DID WELL:

WHAT AM I LOOKING FORWARD TO?

_____

_____

_____

_____

THINGS I AM GRATEFUL FOR:

1. _____

2. _____

3. _____

4. _____

5. _____

6. _____

7. _____

Daily Gratitude Practice

DATE: _____   S M T W R F S

WHAT INSPIRED ME TODAY?

_____

_____

_____

_____

A MOMENT THAT MADE ME SMILE:	SOMETHING I DID WELL:

WHAT AM I LOOKING FORWARD TO?

_____

_____

_____

_____

THINGS I AM GRATEFUL FOR:

1. _____
2. _____
3. _____
4. _____
5. _____
6. _____
7. _____

Strengthening Optimism with Mantras

Mantras are a way to focus your mind and strengthen that which you set your mind to. Let them remind you of the power you hold.

Exercise: Harnessing Optimism
Highlight the following lines that resonate with you, add your own and revisit them whenever you want a boost.

On Choosing Optimism
- I focus on what I can control and let go of what I can't.
- My challenges are opportunities to grow stronger and wiser.
- I choose hope over fear and action over despair.

On Building Resilience
- Every setback is a setup for a comeback.
- I am strong, capable and ready to take on life's challenges.
- Resilience is my superpower; I bounce back stronger every time.

On Gratitude
- I am grateful for this moment and all it offers.
- My life is full of blessings, big and small.
- Gratitude fuels my optimism and inspires my actions.

On Empowerment:
- I am the author of my own story, and my next chapter is bright.
- I am capable of creating the life I want.
- Good things are waiting for me, and I am ready to receive them.

Cultivating Optimism
Words to Live By

Distinguishing Between Optimism & Magical Thinking

Optimism and magical thinking may seem similar at first glance, but they're fundamentally different. Optimism is rooted in effort and reality, inspiring action and progress. Magical thinking, on the other hand, is grounded in fantasy and avoidance, offering false hope without the work required to bring meaningful change.

Exercise: Optimism vs. Magical Thinking
This exercise is designed to help you reflect on your current mindset, distinguish optimism from magical thinking, and build a realistic, optimistic foundation for moving forward.

While the following chapters will guide you in identifying your life goals and creating a detailed roadmap, this exercise focuses on strengthening your optimistic perspective and refining your plans for daily trials and shorter-term goals.

Step 1: List Your Current Challenges and Goals
1. **Challenges:** Write down the obstacles or difficulties you're currently facing.
2. **Goals:** Identify your goals or desired outcomes.
3. **Solutions:** Outline realistic steps you're taking or plan to take to overcome these challenges or reach your goals.

Step 2: Reflect with Evaluative Questions
1. Am I addressing my challenges directly (optimism) or avoiding them (magical thinking)?
2. Are my goals realistic and achievable (optimism) or overly idealistic (magical thinking)?

3. Am I learning from setbacks and adjusting (optimism) or ignoring failure as a possibility (magical thinking)?
4. Do I understand that success requires effort (optimism) or expect quick results with little work (magical thinking)?
5. Am I consistently working toward my goals (optimism) or waiting passively for change (magical thinking)?
6. Am I adaptable and willing to pivot (optimism) or fixated on one specific outcome (magical thinking)?
7. Am I owning my role in outcomes (optimism) or blaming others (magical thinking)?

Step 3: Make Adjustments if Needed
If you recognize magical thinking in your approach, revisit your plans to align them with a relentlessly optimistic mindset:

1. **Refine Your Plan:** Break down your goals into manageable, actionable steps.
2. **Identify Resources:** Determine what support or tools you need to move forward.
3. **Reset Expectations:** Ensure your goals and timeline are realistic.
4. **Focus on Your Power:** Channel your energy into what you can control.

By grounding your efforts in realistic optimism, you'll stay resilient, focused and empowered to achieve your goals.

Optimism vs Magical Thinking

Using the questions in the previous section, fill in the following chart. Determine if you are employing optimism or magical thinking and what adjustments you may need to make to your plan.

Challenge/Goal:		
Solution/Plan:		
Circle One:	Optimism	Magical Thinking
Edits/ Adjustments:		

Challenge/Goal:		
Solution/Plan:		
Circle One:	Optimism	Magical Thinking
Edits/ Adjustments:		

Challenge/Goal:		
Solution/Plan:		
Circle One:	Optimism	Magical Thinking
Edits/ Adjustments:		

Challenge/Goal:		
Solution/Plan:		
Circle One:	Optimism	Magical Thinking
Edits/ Adjustments:		

Challenge/Goal:		
Solution/Plan:		
Circle One:	Optimism	Magical Thinking
Edits/ Adjustments:		

Challenge/Goal:		
Solution/Plan:		
Circle One:	Optimism	Magical Thinking
Edits/ Adjustments:		

Challenge/Goal:		
Solution/Plan:		
Circle One:	Optimism	Magical Thinking
Edits/ Adjustments:		

Chapter 27: Finding Joy & Strength in the Face of Adversity

Relentless optimist or not, sometimes life is hard.

If you're living through a difficult time right now, ask yourself: Are you surviving, or are you thriving? The answer might change from day to day, and that's okay.

During the almost 15 years I spent enduring challenging times, there were days when just surviving felt like a victory. Sometimes, simply getting through the day is an incredible act of strength.

But there were other days when I found joy, tapped into my strength and took small but meaningful steps that eventually transformed my entire world.

Surviving vs. Thriving

Life, like healing, is rarely linear. It often feels like two steps forward and one step back … and sometimes even two steps forward, three steps back. You're not alone in that – it's just the nature of growth and change.

When you're in survival mode, it's okay to do the bare minimum. Rest and healing are productive, too. If your soul needs a quiet day in a bookstore, curled up in an armchair with a coffee, give yourself permission to do that. If the couch, the park or a friend's comforting presence calls to you, listen. If you need to stay in bed all day, that's fine too.

Do whatever you need to do to get through the day. And when you're ready, splash some water on your face and take the next step forward.

When I was in survival mode, I often found solace in simple tasks. After dropping Aiden off at school, I'd spend my day organizing and decluttering … or sometimes, shopping and re-cluttering. These activities didn't directly impact my future, but they brought me peace in the storm. That peace improved my outlook, and over time, that outlook shaped my decisions and my path forward.

People often say the difference between surviving and thriving is all about mindset. I think it's more nuanced than that, but I do agree it begins there.

When you're surviving, you're focused on simply getting through the day. And we've all been there.

When you're thriving, however, you're actively working toward a better future. Thriving means identifying ways to improve your situation and taking action — whether that's learning a new skill, practicing self-care, building your network or simply seeking finding small moments of joy to build upon.

Finding Joy in the Ordinary
"Find joy in the ordinary?" you may ask. "Even in hard times?"

Yes. Especially in hard times.

Start with small moments of joy and let them grow into a foundation of strength. Seek out tiny wins: a perfectly brewed cup of coffee, your favorite song on the radio or sunlight streaming through the trees just so. These moments may feel insignificant, but over time, they can transform your mindset.

Let these moments create a snowball effect, where small joys strengthen your inner reserves, bolster your motivation, fuel your optimism and empower you to move forward.

For me, ladybugs have always been a touchstone of hope, a symbol of good fortune. When I consciously look for the fortunate things in life, I tend to notice and appreciate them more.

Red cardinals are another powerful symbol for me. They remind me of my grandmother and aunts who have passed, a sign of their enduring presence and love. When I see a cardinal, I feel their strength and support, and that encourages me to find strength within myself.

What are your touchstones, your symbols of hope? What symbols or reminders help you pause and focus on the positive, even for a moment?

Reframing your thinking to seek out the good isn't always easy, especially during hard times. But when you can shift your focus, even briefly, it can make all the difference.

Even during the worst times, when my home life was in complete turmoil, I would remind myself that the world is full of good people. It wasn't always easy to believe, but it was a truth I kept returning to.

Rya Hazelwood | 167

Life can feel overwhelming, even impossible at times, but with the right mindset and deliberate actions, you are capable of overcoming anything.

The Power of Positive Self-Talk

Life is full of highs and lows, and the only constant is change. Through it all, your inner voice is your most powerful tool.

How are you talking to yourself?

Speak to yourself with kindness and positivity. When self-doubt or criticism creeps in, acknowledge it and then let it go.

Try this visualization: Picture your mind as a tree filled with leaves. Your negative thought is written on one of those leaves, fluttering in the wind. Now, watch that leaf fall from the tree's boughs. See it float down a stream, and wave it goodbye as it drifts out to sea.

Even small shifts in phrasing can make a significant impact as you rework your thinking. Don't let life happen *to* you – reframe it so life happens *for* you.

One small shift in thinking made a dramatic difference for me, and it boils down to the words "have to" and "get to."

"I have to go to work today" becomes "I get to go to work today." Suddenly, work is no longer a burden but a privilege.

"I'm so tired, and I still have to give Jacob a bath" becomes "I get to give Jacob a bath." Instead of feeling weighed down by exhaustion, I felt grateful for the moments I got to share with him.

Try it:

"I get to read to my son. I get to fill his love tank. I get to have this quiet time to help him feel safe and cherished."

Suddenly it's a blessing.

"I get to take care of myself."

"I get to go for a run."

"I get to go to class."

"I get to go to the store."

"I get to be present for my loved ones."

"I get to reframe my thinking."

"I get to make new choices."

"I get to learn and grow from this experience."

"I get to embrace this challenge."

"I get to explore new opportunities."

"I get to invest in my future."

"I get to practice gratitude."

"I get to create the life I want."

"I get to build a better future."

"I get to."

Each shift reframes a challenge into an opportunity and a task into a blessing.

Exercise: Reframing Your Thinking
Shifting your mindset can transform the way you approach challenges and opportunities. This two-part exercise is designed to help you reflect deeply and practice quick, impactful shifts in perspective.

1. **Reflective Questions:** Explore the prompts provided in the Reframing Your Thinking Worksheet to gain insights and uncover areas of growth. Take your time with each question – there are no wrong answers.
2. **Quick Mindset Shifts:** Practice reframing your thoughts in real time using the "I get to" principle. Refer to the Positive Mindset Shifts Worksheet to write your own reframed thoughts. This exercise will help you move from a place of obligation or frustration to one of gratitude and opportunity.

Final Thoughts
Life can be hard, but you are capable of incredible strength and resilience. Start small. Find joy in the ordinary. Reframe your thinking.

Day by day, step by step, you'll move from surviving to thriving and build the life you deserve.

Reframing Your Thinking

This worksheet can be applied to any number of feelings, situations or tasks in your life. Use these questions to help you reframe your thinking and turn what feels like a burden into an opportunity for growth or joy. I encourage you to return to this worksheet whenever you need a mental reset.

Once you've answered the questions, list any thoughts or concepts that you've successfully reframed.

Reflect on Your Current Mindset

What is something that you used to see as a chore but now see as a privilege?

How did reframing your thinking about it change your experience?

How can you apply this shift in perspective to your current situation?

Identify Opportunities

What hidden opportunities does this task or situation offer?

How can accomplishing this task improve your overall happiness?

In what ways could completing this help or support your loved one(s)?

What skills, strengths or abilities can you sharpen by going through this process?

Explore Joy and Accomplishment

Where can you find small moments of joy in this task or situation?

Will accomplishing this bring you a sense of pride or fulfillment?

How might your attitude change if you view this as a privilege rather than an obligation?

Consider the Positive Impacts

What positive effects will completing this task or process have on you?

What positive effects could it have on others?

How will your future self benefit from accomplishing this?

Next Steps

Now that you've reflected on these questions, list one action you can take today to reframe a current situation and approach it with a more positive mindset. Remember, each small shift in thinking builds toward greater resilience and joy.

Additional Thoughts

Use this space to jot down any further insights, reflections or thoughts as you work through reframing your mindset.

Reframing Your Thinking

Positive Mindset Shifts

I have to.	→	I get to.
Life happens to you.	→	Life happens for you.
I've made a mistake.	→	I've learned a lesson.
Flawed.	→	Flawesome.
	→	
	→	
	→	
	→	
	→	
	→	
	→	
	→	
	→	
	→	
	→	

Chapter 28: Your Village

I've shared how vital my support network was in helping me face, survive and ultimately escape the challenges of my relationships with Chad and Trip. Yet, it wasn't until I found myself in dire need of that support that I truly realized the depth and strength of my village.

It's not that my village hadn't always been there. It had. The truth was, I simply hadn't allowed myself to lean on it. Asking for help has always been difficult for me, and I didn't reach out until I hit a breaking point.

My advice to you? Don't wait that long.

What I learned was this: the people who love you want to help. They don't see you as a burden; they're relieved to be let in. They're eager to offer support, and they will hold you together when you feel like you're falling apart.

Building a village isn't always straightforward, especially when you've been isolated by someone who seeks to sever your connections. In fact, I moved away from my village – distancing myself from my support system – before finally finding my way back.

You see, a hallmark of narcissistic abuse is the systematic separation of a victim from their support network, and Chad's actions were no exception.

As I mentioned previously, Chad rarely engaged at family events himself and made it uncomfortable if I did. He would berate me or punish me with the silent treatment if I dared to interact, have too much fun or shine too brightly.

One example stands out vividly in my memory.

It was a November evening, and we were celebrating my youngest sister's 30th birthday. The night was magical: friends, family, twinkle lights and Prosecco. It was the most fun I had had, and the most connected I had felt to my family, in as long as I could remember.

We talked, we laughed, we bonded.

Chad, however, sulked. First in the house, then on the front steps, and finally, in his car, on a texting tirade. His complaints escalated until they pulled me away from the party.

On the 45-minute drive home, he criticized me relentlessly, calling me an embarrassing wife, an irritating sister and the lowlight of the evening. By the time we reached home, I was a wreck, crying and questioning everything.

I was confused and humiliated. I felt horrible, thinking I had somehow ruined my sister's birthday. I had thought everyone was having a wonderful time ... had I been so wrong?

I am typically confident and successful in social settings. "But if my husband is telling me how awful I was, then it must be true," I thought.

The next morning, I texted my sister, apologizing profusely.

"What are you talking about?" she replied. "Everyone loved you. We had so much fun!"

Relieved but shaken, I began to tread carefully at family gatherings, afraid of Chad's criticism. Over time, my once-vibrant connections faded into cautious distance.

When I finally began to free myself from Chad's manipulation and gaslighting, my confidence in my relationships had eroded. I felt broken and disconnected. But I also knew I desperately needed my family and friends.

Rebuilding my village was neither an immediate nor deliberate process. I didn't wake up one day and think, "I'll rally my loved ones today." But maybe I should have.

Because of the division Chad had created, I felt insecure leaning on my village. So, I started small, sharing my truths with one person at a time. With every conversation, my confidence grew, and my willingness to reach out expanded. Each person responded with love, support and perspective, helping me rebuild my trust in both them and myself.

And with each conversation, my village took shape.

Ultimately, when I needed them the most, my network enveloped me without hesitation. Reaching out to my loved ones changed everything. And I realized that they had been there all along, I just had to let them in.

As I opened up to my trusted circle about Chad's narcissism, abuse and infidelity, I gained perspective and strength. I shared my shock, my emotional turmoil and my feelings of doubt, grief and anger. And each person I leaned on gave me what I needed in their own way – from validation, insights and advice to love, encouragement and hope.

And they shared their own stories.

Remember, I was naïve about narcissists and the hallmarks of that kind of abuse. It was a revelation to learn that three of my friends had survived narcissistic relationships. And their experiences helped me see the truth of my own situation. They helped clear the haze of gaslighting and manipulation.

"Tell me the hard truths," I would say. And they did.

They sent me articles and resources that fed my education in narcissism and trauma bonds. They reminded me that I was not alone, and that hope and happiness were waiting on the other side.

And now, standing on the proverbial other side, I can assure you that there is so much hope and happiness to be had. The journey may not be easy, but I promise you, it's worth it.

So, who is in your village? Who are your trusted confidants? Who are your most fervent supporters? Who loves you?

If you haven't already, I encourage you to reach out. Start with one person. Share your truths and let them support you. From there, add who you need when you need them. Let your village hold you up and hold you together.

And if you feel like you can't rely on people already in your life, there are other resources. Find a counselor. Join a support group, either online or in person. Are you part of a church? What resources do they offer? Would Al-Anon or a similar organization be helpful for you?

When I was struggling with Trip's addiction, I attended an Al-Anon meeting for loved ones of alcoholics. While I was not a regular participant, that group gave me valuable perspective. Additionally, Al-Anon's Three Cs both empowered and comforted me: "I didn't cause it, I can't control it, and I can't cure it."

I also joined a private group on Facebook for family members of alcoholics and found that to be informative and supportive. Finally, there are many content creators across social media and beyond who focus on recognizing and recovering from narcissistic abuse and trauma bonds.

While I caution against believing everything you see online, many of these resources can be valuable. They offer encouragement, share truths and provide insights.

So, however you can, wherever you can, seek community and build your village. It will make all the difference.

Building Your Village: Inspiration Sheet

Your village is your foundation: the network of people who lift you up, stand by your side and make life's challenges a little easier to bear. Building and strengthening your village is one of the most powerful steps you can take on your journey toward a thriving, balanced life.

Use these steps as inspiration to reflect on your current village and discover ways to grow and nurture your support system.

1. **Identify Your Support System:** Who do you turn to for advice, comfort or encouragement? These people form the foundation of your village, your lifeline in times of need and your cheerleaders in moments of joy.
2. **Define What You Need:** Consider where you could use more support. Be clear about the kind of help you're seeking.
3. **Expand Your Network:** Seek opportunities to meet new people and grow your circle. Local groups, hobby clubs or online communities can be great places to connect. I met some amazing friends through a local mommy group, which became my lifeline when Aiden was a baby.
4. **Strengthen Your Connections:** Focus on depth, not numbers. Open up, communicate honestly and ensure the relationship is mutually supportive. Strong connections are built with effort and authenticity.
5. **Be Open to New People:** You never know when someone may enter your life and become a key part of your support system. Stay open to new people and experiences; they may bring unexpected blessings.

6. **Give Back to Your Village:** Villages thrive on reciprocity. Share your time, skills and knowledge with others. Supporting your village not only strengthens those relationships but also brings fulfillment to your own life.
7. **Embrace Diversity:** A resilient village is made up of people with different perspectives and backgrounds. Stay curious and open-minded, as diverse viewpoints enrich your support system and make it stronger.
8. **Ask for Help When You Need It:** Your village can't support you if they don't know you need it. Be honest about your struggles and trust those who care about you to show up for you.
9. **Celebrate Successes**: Be genuinely happy for your village's achievements and celebrate their milestones. Positivity breeds trust and strengthens the bonds you share.
10. **Express Gratitude:** Show appreciation for your village. A simple thank you, a kind note or a heartfelt gesture can go a long way in maintaining and deepening your connections.

Final Thoughts
Building and nurturing your village is an ongoing process, one that requires intention, openness and effort. Be deliberate in strengthening your relationships, stay receptive to new connections and don't hesitate to lean on those who care about you.

Your village is your foundation, your refuge and your greatest resource. It can make all the difference on your journey. And when the time comes, you'll find yourself standing on the other side of life's challenges, stronger and more connected than ever before.

Exercise: Build Your Village

Take some time to reflect on the people in your life who support, inspire and encourage you. This exercise will help you identify the strengths of your current village, pinpoint areas where you need more support and begin intentionally building a network that helps you thrive.

1. **Identify Your Current Network:** Write down the names of family, friends, mentors, colleagues or others who offer support or encouragement.
2. **Assess Your Needs:** Think about where you could use more support. Are there specific areas of your life where a stronger network would make a difference?
3. **Add to Your Village:** Over time, look for opportunities to connect with new people who align with your values or goals. Expanding your village can open doors to fresh perspectives and deeper connections.

Create Your Village Contact Sheet

Think of this as a moment to pause and intentionally recognize the people in your life who make up your village. Use the following pages to list their names and contact information for easy access.

You might already have these names saved in your phone or jotted down elsewhere but compiling them in one place ensures that when life feels heavy or overwhelming, you know exactly who to turn to.

This isn't just about writing names; it's about acknowledging the people who are there for you – the ones who lift you up, encourage you and remind you of your strength.

My Village

My Trusted Confidants, Allies and Loved Ones

Name   Phone

Email

Name   Phone

Email

Name   Phone

Email

Name   Phone

Email

Name   Phone

Email

Name   Phone

Email

Name   Phone

Email

Name   Phone

Email

Name   Phone

Email

Name   Phone

Email

Name   Phone

Email

Name   Phone

Email

Name   Phone

Email

Name   Phone

Email

Name   Phone

Email

Name   Phone

Email

Name   Phone

Email

Name   Phone

Email

Name   Phone

Email

Name   Phone

Email

Name   Phone

Email

Name   Phone

Email

Name   Phone

Email

Name   Phone

Email

Chapter 29: Knowing When Enough is Enough

Enough is a feeling, not an amount.

Enough happens when your situation no longer serves you and something has to change. Sometimes, it comes in the form of a rock-bottom breaking point, as it did for me. But it doesn't always have to. Enough is simply enough. And when you feel it, you'll know.

Easier said than done. Believe me, I know that all too well.

So, how do you recognize when enough is truly enough? How do you go from living in unhappiness to taking those big, life-changing steps? How do you know?

In both of my past marriages, I waited too long. I unintentionally held on until catastrophic events forced my hand. I waited for the kind of undeniable, in-your-face moment that made it impossible to stay.

In hindsight, it's easy to see where I went wrong. Now, years later, I try to be grateful for the lessons learned and the person I became through the hardships. But in the thick of it, adopting that mindset was so much harder.

With Trip, "enough" came after a cascade of moments all in the span of a few weeks: the day he didn't pick Jacob and me up from the hospital; his second DUI; and the scuffle on the stairs over his keys. With Chad, it was the brutal confirmation of his affair with Becky.

Both situations were riddled with red flags long before those final breaking points. And yet, I stayed.

Why? What kept me in for too long? Why did I ignore the signs and prolong the pain?

There were many reasons, some of which we've explored. One of the biggest was the benefit of the doubt, a value I hold dear and still believe in. However, I've learned the hard way that giving someone the benefit of the doubt can sometimes go too far, crossing into a territory that harms you more than it helps.

I still believe that with mutual respect, communication, shared values and love, almost any relationship issue can be resolved – as long as both people are willing. It's not easy; it requires effort and sacrifice on both sides. But for the right person, it's worth it. (Key phrase: if both people are willing.)

However, there are three things I know now that I cannot and will not tolerate, and they are my hard-stop dealbreakers: adultery, addiction and abuse.

Unfortunately, I've encountered all three. In the past, I excused behaviors and clung to false hope, staying far longer than I should have. Knowing what I know now, I would act swiftly and decisively if faced with any of these again.

I still believe in giving the benefit of the doubt. But it cannot be given unconditionally or endlessly. At some point, people stop deserving your trust. And they stop deserving a place in your life.

So, what is your "enough?" What are your deal breakers? Are they present in your current situation?

If your safety or well-being is at risk, I urge you to seek help and leave immediately. But if your situation is not as clear-cut, ask yourself: What are your reasons for staying?

Is your situation fixable? Do you share love, trust and kindness? Are your needs being met? Is your communication healthy and effective? Are the challenges ones you can work on together? Does the idea of finding a solution fill you with hope — and is that hope grounded in reality, not magical thinking?

If your relationship has a foundation of love, respect and the potential for growth, then put in the effort. Do the work. No relationship is perfect. We all make compromises and face frustrations. Those are part of any healthy partnership.

Further, there is no one-size-fits-all solution. Every person and situation is unique. We each face our storms with different resources and in different boats.

For me, as frightening as it was to leave Trip and be a single mom, and as heart-wrenching as the end was with Chad, the reality of staying was worse.

You can love someone and still not want them in your life. You can love someone and still let them go. You can love someone and still choose yourself. In fact, you should choose yourself.

Sometimes, the healthiest way to love someone is from afar. As difficult as it may be, letting go can be the most loving act ... for them and for you.

Your happiness is your responsibility. Likewise, you cannot be responsible for someone else's happiness. Trip once told me that, as his wife, it was my job to make him happy. But happiness isn't something you can give to another person. It comes from within.

A thriving relationship divides grief and multiplies joy, but that only happens when both people take ownership of their own emotional well-being.

For your sake, and the sake of your current and future relationships, you must prioritize yourself. Make decisions that lead you toward peace, joy and fulfillment.

So, what would make you happy? Not just in this moment, but deep down in your core? In your vision of the future, what brings you genuine peace and joy?

Change can be terrifying. Sometimes, staying in the familiar, even if it's miserable, feels easier. And it may be, in the short term. But at what cost?

You will know – and perhaps only you will know – when enough is finally enough. Only you can define it for yourself, and only you can decide when it's time to move forward. But when that moment comes, you'll be ready. You'll either be ready to leave or ready to do the work to make positive changes, but you will be ready.

Whatever you choose, trust in your strength and know that brighter days are ahead.

Exercise: Define Your "Enough"
Enough is deeply personal: a feeling, not a fixed point. Recognizing when a situation no longer serves you is about trusting your instincts. It's not about reaching a specific milestone but rather it's about tuning into yourself, your situation and your gut.

Take this opportunity to reflect on your current situation and define what "enough" looks like for you. Use the questions on the following pages to gain clarity on your current situation and your unique sense of enough, and to start shaping your vision for a positive way forward.

Remember, enough is a personal feeling. Trust yourself to know when it's time to make a change.

Reflection Worksheet

This worksheet is designed to help you identify your breaking point and evaluate whether "enough is enough" in your current situation. Take your time answering these questions honestly and thoughtfully. Your responses will help you gain clarity and take meaningful steps toward change.

Identifying the Core Issue

What is the primary challenge or issue in your current situation? (Is it a relationship, job or something else?)

Are you feeling fulfilled and happy in this, or do you constantly find yourself questioning if it's worth it?

How long have you been feeling unhappy or unsure? When was the last time you felt happy or satisfied?

Recognizing Your "Enough"

What behaviors, circumstances or patterns have made you question whether you've reached your limit?

Are any of your dealbreakers being crossed? (Examples: trust, respect, loyalty, communication, abuse, etc.)

How is this situation affecting your mental and emotional well-being?

Do you still have hope for a positive outcome?

Assessing Your Reasons for Staying

Why are you staying in this situation? (Be honest — are you staying out of fear, comfort, loyalty, hope for change, etc.?)

Have you tried to communicate your feelings and concerns? What are some steps you can take to improve the situation before making a decision?

When you use effective communication, does your partner hear you and respond with understanding or with defensiveness?

What are the benefits of staying? What are the costs of staying?

Defining Your Dealbreakers

What are your personal dealbreakers? (e.g., dishonesty, addiction, neglect, abuse, etc.)

Are those dealbreakers present in your current situation?

If your dealbreakers are present, why do you feel hesitant to act on them?

Have you already given this situation multiple chances? If so, what has changed, if anything?

Visualizing the Future

What would your life look like if you chose to stay and work on things? How does that make you feel? Would staying align with your long-term goals and values?

What would your life look like if you chose to leave? How does that make you feel? Would leaving align with your long-term goals and values?

Have you consulted trusted friends or family about their thoughts on the situation? If so, what do they advise?

Taking Ownership of Your Happiness

Are you taking responsibility for your own happiness, or are you waiting for someone else to make you happy?

Do you feel empowered to make changes, or are you still hesitant? Why?

What steps can you take today to either leave or start addressing the core issues in this situation?

Next Steps

Based on your answers, write down one or two concrete steps you can take toward resolving this situation. These can be small but meaningful actions like having an honest conversation, reaching out to your support network or seeking professional help.

Commit to reviewing this worksheet in a month. Has anything changed? Do you still feel the same, or are you closer to finding peace and resolution?

Chapter 30: Putting Your Happiness First

Your happiness is a priority. *You* are a priority.

There's a growing body of research around what makes people truly happy. Experts study smiles and brain activity. They analyze relationships and the importance of human connection. They explore philosophy, religion and how our inner worlds – our self-talk, the light we use to color our memories, and the lenses through which we view the world – shape our sense of self and of joy.

Happiness comes in many forms. It might be found in activities, like playing with your child, laughing with friends, reading a good book or going for a long walk. It might arise from feelings of acceptance, loving or being loved.

But what makes you truly happy at your core? What puts your mind and soul at ease?

At some point in every failed relationship or challenging situation I've faced, I came to a crucial realization: I needed to take an active role in protecting my peace. I've never thrived in drama; it's something I've always wanted to avoid. Unfortunately, life doesn't always give us that choice. Sometimes, we're thrust into the eye of the storm, whether it's one of our own making or someone else's.

Learning to prioritize my happiness didn't come easily. I spent years as a chronic people-pleaser, doing everything I could to keep others happy, often at my own expense. The thought of upsetting someone, even someone who was hurting me, felt unbearable.

For years, I tried to fill other people's buckets, even when they couldn't spare a drop for mine. I would take on disappointment and hurt that weren't mine to bear. I'd make excuses for others just to avoid the discomfort of seeing them unhappy or angry.

But more often than not, trying to be everything for others left me completely drained. With Trip, I bore the heavy burden of his disappointment, illness and anger. With Chad, I twisted myself into knots, desperately trying to meet his impossible expectations and avoid his manipulative outbursts. I spent years trying to anticipate their needs, fix their problems and smooth over every conflict. Yet no matter how much I gave, it was never enough. My bucket was empty while theirs seemed bottomless.

Eventually, I realized that I couldn't hold myself accountable for anyone else's feelings or actions. I had to stop personalizing my loved ones' moods and trust them to take ownership of their own emotions. I could support them, encourage them and offer compassion, but I wasn't responsible for their happiness. I was responsible only for my own choices, emotions and reactions.

That realization led me to one of the hardest lessons of my life: learning how to set and enforce boundaries to protect my peace and prioritize my happiness.

I stopped enabling Trip's drinking and finally stood my ground. I stopped allowing Chad to manipulate me and distort my reality.

Both decisions were difficult to make and even harder to enforce, but they were essential for reclaiming my peace of mind.

Even after my marriage to Chad ended, I still had to navigate his volatile behavior. We were running a business together, so going no-contact wasn't an option. Although the marriage was over, his attempts to control and provoke me were not.

At first, I tried to keep the peace for the sake of the business. I thought that if I accommodated Chad's demands, he would stay cooperative, and the business would thrive. But I was wrong. His outbursts continued, and my efforts to appease him only left me more depleted.

Eventually, I stopped prioritizing his emotional state and started prioritizing my own. I set boundaries, and with each one I set and held, I felt stronger.

My boundaries evolved over time. I began by refusing to engage in personal disputes, limiting my responses to legitimate business matters. Then, I eliminated texting as a communication method, confining our interactions to email and a professional messaging platform. I stopped reacting to his attempts to manipulate me and instead adopted a "gray rock" approach, keeping my responses neutral, brief and uninteresting.

There is something profoundly empowering – and surprisingly effective – about receiving a series of angry emails from someone trying to provoke you and simply replying with one word: "Disagree."

Initially, these changes were hard and terrifying. I dreaded the potential backlash, but I held my ground. Over time, the fear began to fade, replaced by a growing sense of empowerment. Ultimately, the more boundaries I established, the more peace I found.

Chad's behavior didn't change, but my reaction to it did. His mask was off, and behind it was someone who seemed to need to lift himself up by pushing others down. But even that knowledge wasn't an instant cure.

For months after our divorce, even seeing his name in an email or text would trigger my fight-or-flight response. My heart would race as I braced myself, wondering, "What now? What drama do I have to deal with today?"

Over time, though, as I strengthened my boundaries and my commitment to protecting my peace solidified, his once-intimidating tirades and threats became almost laughable. The power plays were exposed as bluster, full of hubris, petty complaints and unreasonable demands. And they stopped affecting me altogether.

His emails and messages, once a source of stress and dread, became little more than noise. Finally, though, I made the decision to sell my half of the company. Our visions for the business no longer aligned, and no amount of potential profit was worth the ongoing stress of dealing with him.

Letting go of that business, what I had once thought was my professional future, was scary … but it was also freeing. And in letting go, I discovered something even better: a new professional passion that filled me with purpose and joy.

Was prioritizing my peace easy? No. Were there guarantees that my new path would succeed? No. But was it worth it? A resounding yes.

If you're struggling to prioritize your own happiness, I want you to know that it's possible. Protecting your peace doesn't happen overnight, but with intentional effort, it's something you can achieve.

So, how can you begin?

There are many ways to personalize this journey for yourself, and in the next section, we'll explore some practical steps to help you get started.

Prioritizing Your Peace and Joy Toolkit

Protecting your peace and prioritizing your happiness requires intentional actions, boundaries and self-compassion. This toolkit – which calls back and builds upon several critical concepts explored so far – is a flexible resource filled with tools and exercises to help you nurture your well-being. It's not a rigid, step-by-step guide but rather a collection of adaptable strategies to support your journey toward inner calm and fulfillment.

Releasing What No Longer Serves You

It's okay to not be okay sometimes. Allow yourself time to sit with your emotions rather than suppressing them. After all, you have to actually *go* through it to *get* through it and ultimately *grow* through it.

1. **Explore the Root Cause:** Ask yourself why you're feeling a certain way. Digging into the underlying reasons can give you insight, helping you to better manage and understand your emotions.
2. **Release Negative Feelings:** Once you've acknowledged and processed these emotions, visualize letting them go. Imagine each feeling as a leaf blowing away in the wind, finally floating out to sea, leaving you lighter and freer.

Visualization can be a powerful tool to help shift your mindset and release what no longer serves you.

Exercise: Feelings Final Call

1. **List:** Write down any unpleasant thoughts or feelings you'd like to release.
2. **Visualize:** Picture each one blowing away like a leaf in the wind, floating far beyond reach.
3. **Release:** Mentally wave each feeling goodbye, leaving space for peace and clarity.

My Worry List

Visualize Each Worry Blowing Away
Like a Leaf in the Wind

_____

_____

_____

_____

_____

_____

_____

_____

_____

_____

_____

_____

_____

_____

_____

_____

Setting and Holding Boundaries

Setting boundaries is essential to protecting your peace. Boundaries are not selfish; they're necessary. When you set boundaries, you're defining what is acceptable in your life and clarifying the actions you'll take if those boundaries are crossed.

1. **The Power of Saying No:** You have every right to say no to anything that doesn't align with your values or bring you joy. It's okay if this disappoints others; prioritizing your well-being is a form of self-respect.
2. **Enforce Your Boundaries:** If someone crosses your boundaries, respond by removing yourself from the situation or limiting their access to you. Remember, the only people upset by your boundaries are those who benefitted from disregarding them.

Exercise: Building Boundaries

1. **Identify Boundaries:** List the boundaries you currently have or want to establish. Be clear and specific about each one.
2. **Define Your Actions:** Outline the steps you'll take if these boundaries are challenged. Knowing your response ahead of time will help you hold firm if and when the moment arises.

My Boundaries

Boundaries to Set and Hold

- ○ _____
- ○ _____
- ○ _____
- ○ _____
- ○ _____
- ○ _____
- ○ _____
- ○ _____
- ○ _____
- ○ _____
- ○ _____
- ○ _____
- ○ _____
- ○ _____
- ○ _____
- ○ _____

Letting Go of Toxic Relationships
Just as with setting boundaries, letting go of toxic relationships is essential for protecting your energy and well-being. This can be difficult, especially when the person is someone you care about. However, prioritizing your own happiness and peace sometimes means creating distance from those who bring harm or negativity into your life.

It's important to remember: You can love someone and still choose not to give them access to you.

Some people are best loved from afar.

Exercise: Toxic Behavior Awareness
1. **Identify:** List the toxic behaviors you will no longer tolerate or enable in your life.
2. **Commit:** Set an intention to remove or distance yourself from relationships that cross these boundaries, knowing you are prioritizing your well-being.

Banned Toxic Behaviors

Behaviors I Will No Longer Tolerate nor Enable

⊘ _____
⊘ _____
⊘ _____
⊘ _____
⊘ _____
⊘ _____
⊘ _____
⊘ _____
⊘ _____
⊘ _____
⊘ _____
⊘ _____
⊘ _____
⊘ _____
⊘ _____
⊘ _____
⊘ _____

Practicing Gratitude

As a continuation of the gratitude exercise in *Chapter 26: Optimism in Action: Beyond Magical Thinking*, this practice will deepen your ability to find joy, even during tough times.

1. **Want What You Have:** Like we explored previously, reframing your thoughts helps you appreciate the blessings in your life. Try replacing "I have to" with "I get to." For instance, instead of thinking, "I have to clean the house," shift to, "I get to create a welcoming space for myself." Gratitude thrives when you see the opportunities within your daily life.

2. **Find Joy in the Small Things:** Gratitude doesn't have to stem from grand milestones or dramatic changes. Often, it's the small, everyday moments that hold the most joy. Recognizing beauty in the ordinary creates lasting peace and fulfillment.

Exercise: Gratitude Reflection Part 2

Building on your gratitude journaling from Chapter 26, take a few moments to reflect on your blessings, diving deeper into your awareness and appreciation.

1. **List:** Write down three things you're grateful for today, no matter how small.
2. **Identify:** Note three things you get to do today. Focus on opportunities rather than obligations.
3. **Reflect:** Consider how each of these gifts, big or small, enriches your life and contributes to your overall well-being.

Gratitude is a powerful tool for finding joy, even in adversity. It reminds you that, despite challenges, there are blessings to be found.

Gratitude Reflection

DATE: ————————————————————————————— S M T W R F S

WHAT I'M THANKFUL FOR TODAY:

1. _____

2. _____

3. _____

TODAY'S OPPORTUNITIES:

1. _____

2. _____

3. _____

REFLECTIONS ON MY GRATITUDE:

_____

_____

_____

_____

_____

_____

_____

_____

_____

_____

_____

Trusting Your Intuition

Trusting your gut is essential for protecting your peace. Your instincts are powerful, yet it's easy to let the benefit of the doubt override your intuition … something I learned to my own detriment. Over time, however, I rediscovered how to trust myself.

A key principle to remember is this: Listen to what people say, but trust what they do. Actions often reveal truths that words try to conceal. You know what's best for yourself, so lean into that inner voice.

But how can you tell if that voice is truly intuition or just anxiety speaking?

Exercise: Differentiating Intuition from Anxiety

When facing a strong feeling or trying to make a decision, it can be challenging to discern whether your reaction or inclination is rooted in anxiety or intuition. Pay attention to how each feels. Anxiety often brings restlessness and discomfort; intuition usually feels calm and grounded even in difficult situations.

Anxiety fixates on "what if" while intuition focuses on "what is." This step-by-step exercise will help you identify the difference:

Step 1: Pause and Breathe

Take a moment to center yourself with deep breaths, focusing on how your body feels. Are you tense or calm? This step creates space to distance yourself from emotional intensity.

Step 2: Identify Physical Sensations

Anxiety and intuition feel different in the body:

- **Anxiety:** Chaotic, with racing heart, tension and restlessness.
- **Intuition:** Calm and steady, a quiet knowing – even in the face of a hard truth.

Ask yourself: Am I feeling agitated or clear and grounded?

Step 3: Reflect on the Source
Consider where the thought or feeling originated:

- **Anxiety:** Stems from fear, overthinking and "what if" scenarios.
- **Intuition:** Comes from present awareness and "what is."

Ask yourself: Am I focused on future fears, or am I grounded in the present?

Step 4: Journal for Clarity
Writing can help bring clarity. Use these prompts to sort through your feelings:

- **Anxiety:** What am I afraid of?
- **Intuition:** What feels true to me right now?

Reflect on whether your responses feel panicked or centered.

Step 5: Seek Perspective
Talk to a trusted friend, advisor or mentor. Share your thoughts and ask if your reactions seem fear-based or grounded.

Step 6: Take a Small Action

If you're still unsure, take a small, low-stakes action related to the situation:

- **Anxiety:** Often diminishes with action, as it thrives on indecision and overthinking.
- **Intuition:** Becomes clearer with confirmation, reinforcing your inner sense of knowing.

With practice, recognizing the difference between anxiety and intuition will become second nature. Use this exercise as a guide whenever you feel uncertain and remember: your body and emotions are invaluable tools for making clear, grounded decisions.

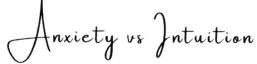

Anxiety vs Intuition

Evaluate any situation currently
on your mind. What does your gut say?
Is it intuition or anxiety?

Anxiety: What If	→	Intuition: What Is
	→	
	→	
	→	
	→	
	→	
	→	
	→	
	→	
	→	
	→	
	→	
	→	
	→	
	→	

Practicing Self-Care
Self-care is essential for maintaining your mental, physical and emotional well-being. It's not about following trends; it's about recharging in ways that genuinely work for you.

1. **Identify What Helps You Recharge:** What brings you joy and relaxation? Whether it's reading, spending time in nature, taking a bath or something else entirely, self-care is unique to each person. Choose activities that feel right for you.
2. **Make Time for Yourself:** Prioritize self-care regularly. Even small acts, like taking a quiet moment for yourself, can help you maintain balance and support your overall well-being.

Exercise: Self-Care Planning
1. **Create:** Make a list of self-care activities that help you relax and feel refreshed.
2. **Integrate:** Aim to include one of these activities in your daily or weekly routine to build consistency in your self-care practice

Self-Care Planner

DATE: _____   S M T W R F S

THINGS THAT MADE ME HAPPY TODAY

- _____
- _____
- _____
- _____

WATER INTAKE

◊◊◊◊ ◊◊◊◊ ◊◊◊◊

32 OZ   64 OZ   96 OZ

SELF-CARE ACTIVITIES

- _____
- _____
- _____
- _____

TODAY'S MOOD

☹ ☹ 😐 ☺ 😃

AFFIRMATIONS

- _____
- _____
- _____
- _____

HABITS TO STOP

_____

_____

_____

HABITS TO START

_____

_____

_____

Seeking Help When You Need It

Asking for help isn't always easy, but it's one of the bravest and most transformative steps you can take. Recognizing when you need support – and knowing where to turn – is a skill, one that can guide you through life's toughest moments.

1. **Reach Out When Necessary:** Your mental and emotional health deserves to be a priority.
2. **Accept That It's Okay to Not Be Okay:** Seeking help is not a weakness. It's a powerful step toward growth, healing and resilience.

Exercise: Build Your Resource List

This isn't just about making a list; it's about equipping yourself for the future. Life's challenges often catch us off guard, and in those moments, it can feel overwhelming to figure out where to turn. Taking the time now to identify resources, from supportive friends to professional organizations, means you'll be prepared when you need it most.

Think of this as creating a safety net. Even if you never need to use it, the process itself is an act of self-care and empowerment.

1. **Create:** Write down the names of people and resources you can turn to for support.
2. **Detail:** Include contact information and note what kind of support they can offer, whether it's a listening ear, expertise or crisis intervention.
3. **Reach Out:** If possible, start connecting with these resources now. Introduce yourself to community groups, find a therapist or counselor and let the people in your life know they're part of your support network.

Resources for Support

People & Resources to Call Upon
When I Need Support

NAME:

Company:

Phone: Email:

Where/How They Help:

NAME:

Company:

Phone: Email:

Where/How They Help:

NAME:

Company:

Phone: Email:

Where/How They Help:

NAME:

Company:

Phone: Email:

Where/How They Help:

NAME:

Company:

Phone: Email:

Where/How They Help:

NAME:

Company:

Phone: Email:

Where/How They Help:

NAME:

Company:

Phone: Email:

Where/How They Help:

NAME:

Company:

Phone: Email:

Where/How They Help:

NAME:

Company:

Phone: Email:

Where/How They Help:

Your Inner Circle of Positivity & Inspiration

The people you surround yourself with in your everyday have a meaningful impact on your life. So, who is in your proverbial boat?

You might already have these names saved in your phone or written in a journal but gathering them all in one place makes it easier to visualize the network of positivity and encouragement you're building. Think of this exercise as more than just writing down contact information. It's a deliberate acknowledgment of the people who are in your corner and an opportunity to consider if there's anyone else you'd like to invite into your boat.

Energy, enthusiasm and optimism are contagious and, when shared, multiply exponentially. So, I ask again: Who do you want to be? Where do you want to go? And who is in your boat?

Exercise: Create Your "Who's in Your Boat" Roster

This isn't just about writing down names: it's about honoring the people who contribute to your journey and recognizing the vital role a positive, inspiring network plays in your growth.

1. **List Your Crew:** Write down the people who currently support you and align with your values.
2. **Fill in the Gaps:** Include anyone you admire and would like to connect with.
3. **Keep It Dynamic:** This list isn't set in stone. As you grow and your journey evolves, so will your relationships. Add to it, update it and keep it as a living document that reflects the support system you're cultivating.

People in My Boat

People Already in My Boat
And Those I Would Like to Add

NAME:

Company:

Phone: Email:

Trait I Admire:

NAME:

Company:

Phone: Email:

Trait I Admire:

NAME:

Company:

Phone: Email:

Trait I Admire:

NAME:

Company:

Phone: Email:

Trait I Admire:

NAME:

Company:

Phone: Email:

Trait I Admire:

NAME:

Company:

Phone: Email:

Trait I Admire:

NAME:

Company:

Phone: Email:

Trait I Admire:

NAME:

Company:

Phone: Email:

Trait I Admire:

NAME:

Company:

Phone: Email:

Trait I Admire:

Final Thoughts

Protecting your peace is a lifelong journey, evolving as your needs and circumstances change. By setting boundaries, letting go of what no longer serves you, and cultivating gratitude, self-care and supportive relationships, you can create a life grounded in peace and joy.

Prioritizing your happiness is not selfish; it's necessary. When you take care of yourself, you're better equipped to care for others and contribute meaningfully to the world around you.

So, what is one small step you can take today to protect your peace and prioritize your happiness? Remember, each step brings you closer to the life you desire.

Chapter 31: Your Roadmap to Change

We ended the last chapter with three powerful questions: Who do you want to be? Where do you want to go? And who is in your boat?

Close your eyes for a moment. Envision your ideal future – one year from now, five years from now. Where are you? Who is with you? What are you doing? Are you safe? Are you happy? Are you whole?

When I was in the middle of my marriage to Trip, my vision looked something like this: "In five years, Trip will be sober, the boys will be happy, and we'll spend our free time traveling." I pictured us as a happy family exploring London, Madrid and Paris: two joyful parents and two happy kids.

Magical thinking.

What I didn't bring into that vision was the reality of Trip's alcoholism and anger. I didn't picture the nights he'd stumble intoxicated through unfamiliar cities, maybe making it back to the hotel, maybe not. I didn't include the pit in my stomach every time he ordered his first drink of the day or the stress of exploring those cities alone with the kids while Trip "slept it off."

I envisioned a Hallmark-movie future when my reality was anything but.

It took me a long time to reconcile that fantasy with the truth. I had to face the harsh reality that things weren't going to magically become a picture of marital and familial bliss. Those fantasies helped me cope in the moment, but they also delayed the difficult choices I needed to make to truly create a better future.

So, I ask again: Where are you now? In your current reality, where will you be in five years? In your ideal reality, where do you want to be?

Now comes the hard question: How can you get there?

Reflection and Pride
Before we dive into the steps ahead, let's take a moment to acknowledge and celebrate everything you've already achieved. Whether these accomplishments span the last few years or the past few days, it's important to pause and reflect. Ask yourself: What am I proud of?

Exercise: Record Your Accomplishments
Make a list of your achievements, big or small. It could be something as simple as getting out of bed each morning or as transformative as making a major life change. What have you accomplished that deserves acknowledgment?

Don't filter yourself – write down everything that comes to mind.

My Accomplishments

Points of Pride Big & Small

_____

_____

_____

_____

_____

_____

_____

_____

_____

_____

_____

_____

_____

_____

_____

_____

Now, take a look at your list. See what you've already done?

Whether through baby steps or big strides, each item represents a moment of resilience, strength or progress. These are your reminders that you're capable of achieving great things, one step at a time.

Draw strength from those facts as you prepare to take the next steps forward.

Action Planner: Creating Your Roadmap

Achieving your goals is a journey that requires both vision and action. It's easy to feel overwhelmed when the path ahead looks long or uncertain. But breaking it down into smaller, manageable steps can make the process feel achievable.

Remember the old adage: "How do you eat an elephant? One bite at a time."

When the path ahead feels overwhelming, don't stress about conquering it all at once. Break it down into smaller, achievable steps. You can't eat a whole elephant in one sitting. Instead, address one element – take that first bite – and then move on to the next until, finally, the elephant is gone.

Let's create your roadmap by breaking down your journey into bite-sized actions, helping you stay focused and make consistent progress.

Step 1: Define Your Goals

You've already begun exploring your goals in earlier sections. Now, take it a step further by writing down your dreams and vision in detail. Be specific about what you want, so you can create a clear picture of where you're headed.

Exercise: Brainstorming Your Future

Use the prompts in the following pages to help you envision and clarify your goals.

Dream big and be honest about what truly brings you joy and fulfillment. This is your chance to articulate the life you want to create.

Defining My Goals

Brainstorming Prompts

What is your ultimate dream or life goal?

What specific achievements are most meaningful to you?

Was there a defining moment or experience that sparked your passion or clarified your life's direction?

How do you personally define success — in your career, relationships or personal growth?

What core values and principles do you want to guide your major life decisions?

Where do you envision yourself at the end of this journey — professionally, emotionally and personally?

What legacy do you want to leave behind? And what stories do you hope your grandchildren will tell about you?

Additional thoughts or reflections:

Step 2: Create a Roadmap

Now that you've defined your goals, it's time to outline the major steps needed to achieve them. Think of your roadmap as a guiding framework: a tool to keep you focused, motivated and on track. Each step builds momentum, bringing you closer to realizing your vision.

What does a roadmap look like?

Following are some examples of broad-stroke roadmaps to inspire you. Let these high-level outlines provide inspiration and serve as a foundation for breaking your goals into smaller, actionable steps (which we'll explore in detail in the following sections).

Example Roadmap: Publishing a Novel
1. Outline your story and key elements (characters, plot, setting).
2. Write a draft (e.g., one chapter per week).
3. Proofread and revise your manuscript.
4. Share the manuscript for feedback.
5. Make changes and finalize your manuscript.
6. Research publishers and submit proposals (or explore self-publishing).
7. Publish – bring your book to life! Celebrate your hard work and success!

Example Roadmap: Planning a Career Change
1. Research potential fields that align with your skills and interests.
2. Update your resume and LinkedIn profile.
3. Enroll in relevant courses or training programs.
4. Network with professionals in your desired field.
5. Apply to job opportunities that excite you.
6. Prepare for interviews and refine your pitch.
7. Land the job and celebrate the transition.

Example Roadmap: Starting a Business
1. Define your business concept and goals.
2. Write a business plan (business model, financial projections, marketing strategy, etc.).
3. Register your business and obtain the necessary licenses.
4. Secure funding to support your startup.
5. Develop and refine your product or service.
6. Create a strategy to reach your target audience.
7. Launch your business.
8. Build your team as needed to support your growth.

Example Roadmap: Divorce and Building a Better Life
1. Define what you want emotionally, financially and logistically.
2. Lean on friends, family, a therapist and legal/financial advisors for guidance.
3. Gather financial records, custody documents and other key paperwork.
4. File or respond to divorce proceedings with your attorney, addressing custody and asset division.
5. Establish clear communication rules with your ex, especially if co-parenting.
6. Open individual accounts, create a budget and stabilize your finances.
7. Focus on self-care, therapy and emotional recovery.
8. Set personal and professional goals aligned with the life you want.
9. Reconnect with hobbies, build new routines and explore opportunities.
10. Honor your growth and the resilience that brought you here.

Disclaimer: These examples are for inspiration only and are not a substitute for professional or legal advice. Consult licensed professionals for personalized guidance related to your specific goals.

Your roadmap doesn't need to be perfect, and it's not set in stone. Life is unpredictable, and adjustments are part of the process. Focus on consistent progress rather than perfection. With dedication, your dreams are absolutely achievable.

Exercise: Sketch Your Roadmap

It's time to create your personalized roadmap. Start by identifying the key milestones that will help you move forward. Even if the full path isn't clear yet, outlining the big steps will give you a visual guide to stay motivated and organized.

Here are some tips:

- **Be Specific:** Define clear goals and milestones.
- **Be Realistic:** Ensure your steps are achievable based on your resources.
- **Be Flexible:** Allow room to adjust as you move forward.

Every action builds momentum and brings you closer to your vision. Use this exercise as a foundation to organize your thoughts, maintain focus and turn your aspirations into reality.

My Roadmap

Stop Dreaming and Start Doing

My Goal:

Step 1

Step 2

Step 3

Step 4

Step 5

Step 6

Step 7

Step 8	
Step 9	
Step 10	

ADDITIONAL NOTES:

Step 3: Seek Advice

No one achieves their dreams entirely alone. Once you've defined your goals, reaching out to those with relevant experience or expertise can provide invaluable guidance. These individuals or organizations may already be part of your village or your boat, or they might be new connections you intentionally seek out for their insight.

Learning from others not only saves time and effort but also helps you refine your plans. The key is to be selective and intentional about who you invite into this circle of advisors.

Traits of a Trusted Advisor:
Look for people who:

- Are reliable and consistent in their support.
- Provide advice based on knowledge and experience.
- Respect your privacy and build trust.
- Listen fully and communicate with compassion.
- Prioritize your best interests with honesty and respect.

Exercise: Record Your Trusted Advisors
This exercise goes beyond simply listing names: it's about intentionally identifying people who bring value to your journey. These advisors might already be part of your support system, or they might be new relationships you cultivate to support your specific goals.

Think critically about the qualities you value in those who advise you. It's not about casting a wide net but rather about curating a focused group of people who can provide reliable guidance and encouragement.

Trusted Advisors

My Professional Network

NAME:

Company:

Phone: Email:

Trait I Admire:

NAME:

Company:

Phone: Email:

Trait I Admire:

NAME:

Company:

Phone: Email:

Trait I Admire:

NAME:

Company:

Phone: Email:

Trait I Admire:

NAME:

Company:

Phone: Email:

Trait I Admire:

NAME:

Company:

Phone: Email:

Trait I Admire:

NAME:

Company:

Phone: Email:

Trait I Admire:

NAME:

Company:

Phone: Email:

Trait I Admire:

NAME:

Company:

Phone: Email:

Trait I Admire:

Step 4: Set Priorities (with a Caveat)
Identify what's most important and tackle your top priorities first. But remember, progress doesn't have to be all or nothing. On days when you're feeling overwhelmed or low on energy, shift your attention to smaller, more manageable tasks that still move you forward.

Every action, no matter how small, builds momentum. Even a single step brings you closer to your goals. Some days will allow for big strides; other days, small victories will be enough. Both are meaningful.

Keep this in mind: One bite, one step, one small win … all of it adds up.

Exercise: Putting Priorities into Action
Now that you've clarified your goals and drafted a broad-strokes roadmap, it's time to translate them into focused, achievable steps. The next two worksheets are designed to help you stay organized and on track:

- **Top Priorities and Goals To-Do List:** Use this sheet to outline your main priorities, setting specific tasks and adding deadlines. Breaking down each element of your roadmap into actionable steps will keep you focused and accountable.
- **Action Matrix:** This tool will help you prioritize tasks by urgency and importance, allowing you to make the most of your time and energy. By using the matrix, you'll be able to identify high-priority actions, avoid distractions and keep moving forward effectively.

Let these worksheets serve as part of your roadmap, guiding you through each step toward your goals.

Top Priorities & Goals

Turn Your Dreams into Realities

- [ ] _____ Deadline: _____
- [ ] _____ Deadline: _____
- [ ] _____ Deadline: _____
- [ ] _____ Deadline: _____
- [ ] _____ Deadline: _____
- [ ] _____ Deadline: _____
- [ ] _____ Deadline: _____
- [ ] _____ Deadline: _____
- [ ] _____ Deadline: _____
- [ ] _____ Deadline: _____
- [ ] _____ Deadline: _____
- [ ] _____ Deadline: _____
- [ ] _____ Deadline: _____
- [ ] _____ Deadline: _____
- [ ] _____ Deadline: _____
- [ ] _____ Deadline: _____
- [ ] _____ Deadline: _____

Action Matrix

Use this chart to visualize what tasks take priority and how best to allocate your time and energy.

HIGH IMPACT

QUICK WINS | MAJOR PROJECTS

LOW EFFORT

HIGH EFFORT

FILL-INS | THANKLESS TASKS

LOW IMPACT

Step 5: Take Action

This is the moment where your dreams begin to take shape, not all at once, but step by step, action by action. It's where plans become progress, and aspirations turn into achievements.

By now, you've outlined your roadmap and prioritized the big milestones. But even the clearest plan can feel overwhelming when the journey ahead seems long. That's where a detailed, actionable to-do list becomes your secret weapon ... not just to track your tasks but to overcome the paralysis of "Where do I even begin?"

Think of this as your thought inventory – a way to get everything swirling around in your head down onto paper. This process helps you clear mental clutter and identify specific steps that support your progress, from life-changing goals to simple, meaningful actions like scheduling a break or sending an encouraging message to a friend.

Let's be honest: To-do lists aren't groundbreaking. You've probably made hundreds in your lifetime. But their value isn't just in the list itself; it's in the way they can help you break through moments of overwhelm, turning a mountain into a series of manageable steps.

Here's what I've found: When I feel stuck or frozen by the sheer volume of what needs to get done, sitting down to write out everything helps me regain control. Seeing tasks laid out in front of me – from the big, bold goals to the tiny actions that only take a minute – creates clarity and gives me somewhere to start. It's not just about organization; it's about action. Writing it all down helps me see what I can do next, what I can do today.

Here's an example of one of mine:

To-Dos: Changing My Life

Example To-Do List

- [x] ~~Write a to-do list.~~
- [ ] List what I am most proud of.
- [ ] List my accomplishments
- [ ] Reframe my thinking
- [ ] Change "have to" to "get to"
- [ ] List what I'm grateful for
- [ ] List people who love me
- [ ] Watch my favorite movie
- [ ] Visualize my future
- [ ] Identify what inspires me
- [ ] Rest
- [ ] Journal re: childhood dreams
- [ ] Journal re: one year goals
- [ ] Journal re: five year goals
- [ ] List my motivators for change
- [ ] Make a pros and cons list
- [ ] Read a book

- [ ] List my trusted advisors
- [ ] Dream big
- [ ] Visit my mom
- [ ] Plan a girl's night out
- [ ] Call my sister
- [ ] Practice self-care
- [ ] List steps to achieve my goals
- [ ] Set a deadline
- [ ] Read Relentless Optimism
- [ ] Take my vitamins
- [ ] Set a boundary
- [ ] Go for a walk
- [ ] Realize that I am not alone
- [ ] Celebrate the little things
- [ ] Create a vision board
- [ ] Chase my dreams
- [ ] Live my best life

And on and on.

Notice how the list includes a mix of big-picture goals, smaller tasks and even self-care items? That's the key to making your list work for you. It's not just about checking things off; it's about creating a balance that keeps you moving forward without burning out.

The real magic happens when you cross off that first item. The satisfaction of completing even a small task builds your enthusiasm, making it easier to tackle the next one.

Before you know it, your momentum is carrying you forward, and it's time to create a brand-new list. That's progress in action, the snowball effect of consistent effort.

Exercise: Create Your Progress in Action To-Do List
This exercise is all about getting everything out of your head and onto paper. Take a few moments to brainstorm and list every task, goal or idea on your mind. Include:

- Big-picture goals and milestones (e.g., launch a business, improve your health)
- Medium-term priorities (e.g., update your resume, plan a budget)
- Simple, daily actions (e.g., text a friend, read a chapter of a book)

Keep in mind that your to-do list is a tool, not a test. It's there to support you, not to make you feel guilty for what isn't done yet. Adjust it as needed, celebrate every completed task and remind yourself that every small action builds toward your larger vision. This is progress in action – one task, one step, one victory at a time.

My To-Dos

Dare to Dream, Commit To Do

- [ ] _____
- [ ] _____
- [ ] _____
- [ ] _____
- [ ] _____
- [ ] _____
- [ ] _____
- [ ] _____
- [ ] _____
- [ ] _____
- [ ] _____
- [ ] _____
- [ ] _____
- [ ] _____
- [ ] _____
- [ ] _____
- [ ] _____

- [ ] _____
- [ ] _____
- [ ] _____
- [ ] _____
- [ ] _____
- [ ] _____
- [ ] _____
- [ ] _____
- [ ] _____
- [ ] _____
- [ ] _____
- [ ] _____
- [ ] _____
- [ ] _____
- [ ] _____
- [ ] _____
- [ ] _____

Step 6: Stay Accountable

Accountability is key to maintaining your progress. Whether through journaling, setting deadlines or enlisting an accountability partner, find a method that works for you to stay on track and motivated.

For example, when I was writing this book, I set a goal to write 1,000 words each day. Life happens, of course, and I didn't always meet that target, but I kept returning to it. Eventually, I scheduled a meeting with a mentor, giving myself a firm deadline and an external source of accountability.

Consider using tools like goal trackers, progress charts or even public commitments to stay focused. Whatever method you choose, hold yourself accountable for your progress and celebrate your efforts along the way.

Exercise: Track Your Progress

Use the following goal tracker worksheet to stay organized, accountable and steadily moving forward. List your goals, start date, target end date, motivation and any key learnings along the way.

Whether you're focused on one main objective or managing multiple tasks, this tracker will help you keep your eye on the prize and make consistent progress.

Goal Tracker

Dream Boldly, Act Bravely

GOAL:

_____

_____

MY MOTIVATION: START DATE:

_____   _____

_____   END DATE:

_____   _____

WHAT I LEARNED:

_____

_____

GOAL:

_____

_____

MY MOTIVATION: START DATE:

_____   _____

_____   END DATE:

_____   _____

WHAT I LEARNED:

_____

_____

GOAL:

_____

_____

MY MOTIVATION: START DATE:

_____   _____

_____   END DATE:

_____   _____

WHAT I LEARNED:

_____

_____

GOAL:

_____

_____

MY MOTIVATION: START DATE:

_____   _____

_____   END DATE:

_____   _____

WHAT I LEARNED:

_____

_____

ADDITIONAL THOUGHTS:

GOAL:

_____

_____

MY MOTIVATION: START DATE:

_____

_____   END DATE:

_____

WHAT I LEARNED:

_____

_____

GOAL:

_____

_____

MY MOTIVATION: START DATE:

_____

_____   END DATE:

_____

WHAT I LEARNED:

_____

_____

ADDITIONAL THOUGHTS:

Step 7: Celebrate Your Success

Don't wait for the big milestones to celebrate. Recognize the small victories along the way — they're just as important. Whether it's a quick happy dance in the kitchen, treating yourself to something special or simply pausing to reflect on your progress, make it a habit to mark these achievements.

Each step forward is worth celebrating because it brings you closer to your goal. Acknowledging your progress not only reinforces positive habits but also keeps your momentum strong. Celebrate yourself — you've earned it!

Exercise: Log Your Successes

As you work toward your goals, take time to recognize and record each milestone and achievement, whether big or small. Use this space to list any victories or accomplishments that keep you moving forward.

Tracking these successes reinforces your commitment and boosts motivation as you see how far you've come.

Every milestone matters!

Triumphs Big & Small

☆ _____

☆ _____

☆ _____

☆ _____

☆ _____

☆ _____

☆ _____

☆ _____

☆ _____

☆ _____

☆ _____

☆ _____

☆ _____

☆ _____

☆ _____

Step 8: Give Yourself Grace

Pursuing your goals and making life changes can be challenging, and progress is rarely linear. Along the way, you may encounter setbacks, delays or moments of exhaustion. It's essential to give yourself grace during these times, allowing space to rest, reflect and rejuvenate.

1. **Rest When Needed:** Taking time to rest doesn't mean you're failing; it means you're recharging. Just as a phone needs to be plugged in after a long day, so do you. Push through exhaustion, and burnout follows. Pause, rest and then return with fresh energy.

2. **Acknowledge Small Wins:** Celebrate the small steps you take toward achieving your goals, even when progress feels slow. Each small step is a building block in your journey. And over time, they add up to meaningful change.

3. **Silence the Inner Critic:** Replace negative self-talk with compassion. Reframe "I made a mistake" to "I'm learning." Shift "I should be further along" to "I'm making progress." And remind yourself: "I'm doing my best.""

4. **Accept Setbacks as Part of the Process:** No journey is perfect, and setbacks aren't failures; they're opportunities to learn. Growth often comes through struggle, and each challenge can teach you something valuable for the road ahead.

5. **Remind Yourself That Progress Takes Time:** Big changes don't happen overnight. Patience is key. Trust that each step, no matter how small, is moving you forward.

6. **Take Care of You:** Self-care isn't an indulgence; it's essential to the journey. Give yourself grace by recognizing that you deserve moments of peace and restoration as much as the success you're

working toward. Recharge today, push forward tomorrow and approach each new day with renewed clarity and energy.

Final Thoughts

Your journey won't always be easy, but with clarity, action and persistence, it will be worth it. This roadmap is your guide, but the real power lies within you.

Life rarely follows a straight path, and neither does personal growth. Stay adaptable, celebrate each milestone and know that every small step counts.

And most importantly, trust in your ability to do whatever you set your mind to.

Chapter 32: Stop Dreaming & Start Doing

How do you feel?

Scared? Hopeful? Maybe both? And despite everything – or perhaps because of everything – relentlessly optimistic?

If fear is part of the mix, that's completely natural. Change can be intimidating. But here's what I want you to hold on to: hope and optimism. And remember, you are not alone. I've been there too. It's not easy, but the best things in life rarely are.

Tough decisions are part of life well-lived, though some are more challenging than others. Whether it's leaving a toxic situation, mending a broken relationship, switching careers or chasing a dream, change can feel uncomfortable and overwhelming.

But it can also be life-altering in the best ways.

So how do you actually make that change?

Well, you've already begun. You've evaluated your situation, rallied your village and crafted a plan. But what now?

Now, you do the work.

You summon your courage, your resolve, your determination and your spirit of relentless optimism, and you dive in. Step by step, bite by bite, you "eat the elephant" until you become the person you want to be, living the life you've envisioned.

I've faced many difficult decisions in my life: leaving toxic relationships; building, and later divesting, a business; starting the IVF journey; switching careers; and even writing this book.

I've confronted fear, manipulation, financial insecurity and imposter syndrome. And yes, there were times when the challenges felt like too much and days when my optimism faltered.

But each time, I picked myself back up, dusted off my optimism and determination, and moved forward with my "get to" attitude. I chose to refocus on the opportunities, not the obstacles.

None of it was easy, but every difficult decision I've made has turned out to be the best choice for my personal growth, my well-being and my family's future.

I hope that one day, you'll look back and feel the same.

Practical Advice for Making the Change

Change doesn't happen all at once. It's a series of small, intentional actions that lead to transformation. You may stumble along the way – we all do – but what matters most is that you get back up and keep going. Perfection doesn't exist; persistence is what's important.

Here are some strategies to help you stay the course:

1. **Start Small and Build Momentum:** Break your goals up into manageable steps. As yourself: "What can I do today that will bring me closer to my goal?" Small actions build confidence and create momentum.
2. **Embrace the Discomfort:** Change is rarely comfortable. Lean into the discomfort, knowing it's a sign of growth. Trust that every challenge you face is moving you closer to the life you envision. Discomfort is proof that you're pushing beyond the status quo.
3. **Stay Connected to Your Why:** Keep your "why" front and center. Write it down. Repeat it to yourself. Use it as a reminder when the going gets tough. Your "why" is your North Star – the guide that keeps you moving forward even when doubt creeps in.
4. **Revisit Your Plan:** Your roadmap isn't set in stone. Life is fluid and so is your journey. Adjust your plan as needed but stay committed to your goals. Adaptation isn't failure; it's strategy.
5. **Celebrate Progress:** Recognize and celebrate every win, no matter how small. Each step forward is an achievement worth honoring. These moments reinforce your motivation and remind you of how far you've come. Joy fuels progress.

6. **Lean on Your Village:** Remember, you don't have to do this alone. Reach out to your trusted advisors, friends or support system. Let them lift you up when you need it. Asking for help isn't weakness; it's strength.
7. **Be Kind to Yourself:** Self-compassion is essential. You will have hard days, setbacks and moments of doubt. Give yourself grace, rest when needed and keep going. Progress isn't linear, but every step, even a step back, is part of the journey.

Final Thoughts

The road to change isn't always easy, but it is worth every step.

You've already shown incredible courage by reflecting on your journey, defining your goals and building a plan. Now, it's time to move forward – one step, one day at a time.

Remember, progress doesn't have to be perfect. Every small action brings you closer to the life you're working to create.

You've got this, and you are worth it!

So keep moving forward with relentless optimism. Trust in your strength, your resilience and your ability to shape and create the life you dream of.

Exercise: Your Commitment to Change
A dream without action is just a wish. It's time to stop dreaming and start doing. The work you do today will pave the way to the life you envision.

Take a moment to solidify your commitment to this journey … to seeing it through, even when the path gets hard.

To strengthen this commitment, write two letters to yourself:

To the Future You Facing a Challenge
Write a letter to the version of you who will inevitably encounter moments of doubt, struggle or frustration along this journey. What words of encouragement and reassurance can you offer?

Remind yourself of the strength and courage you've already demonstrated and the progress you've made. What wisdom or advice would you share in that moment of hardship to help yourself stay the course?

Think of this letter as a lifeline – a message of hope, compassion and a reminder of your "why."

To the Future You Living Your Dream Life
Write a letter to the you who has successfully achieved the transformation you're working toward. Picture yourself living the life you've always wanted.

What would you say to celebrate this incredible accomplishment? How would you honor your courage, resilience and persistence in making this change?

Let this letter be a heartfelt acknowledgment of your journey and a testament to the strength it took to reach your goals.

Keep these letters in a safe place. Revisit them whenever you need motivation, a reminder of your purpose or a boost to keep moving forward.

You've already taken the first bold steps toward change, and you are far more capable than you may yet realize.

No matter what, stay the course … **and stay relentless**.

To My Future Self

Words of Encouragement

To My Future Self

Words of Celebration

Epilogue
ONWARD & UPWARD

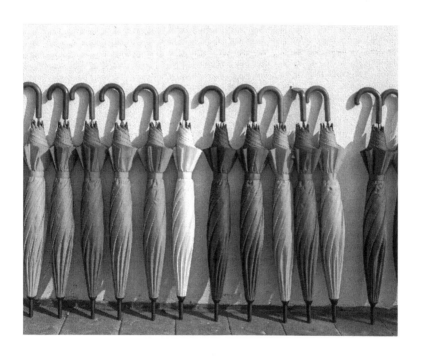

"Go confidently in the direction of your dreams. Live the life you have imagined."
— Henry David Thoreau

Congratulations! You've made it to this point and taken one step – or perhaps many – toward creating a life you truly want to live, thriving under the umbrella of relentless optimism.

During my darkest times, one phrase carried me through: *onward and upward.* It's a mantra that evokes hope, resilience, and of course, relentless optimism.

Henry David Thoreau encapsulates this so eloquently: "Go confidently in the direction of your dreams. Live the life you have imagined."

That's what I've tried to do, and it's my greatest wish for you as well.

So, where did I end up?

Today, I'm living a life I couldn't have imagined 10 years ago … or perhaps wouldn't have dared to imagine.

But I dreamed big, and I worked even harder.

I prioritized peace over a paycheck, discovering that pursuing my own dreams was the most rewarding professional decision I could make.

I summoned all of my courage to write this book. And every time I felt like giving up, I thought about you – the reader I hoped to reach – the person I wanted to pull forward with me, hand in hand, toward a brighter future.

I found a community unlike any I had known before. Once I allowed myself to receive help, my family rallied around me in ways I couldn't even have imagined. And I built a circle of friends who offer me unwavering support and grace.

My boys are healthy and happy, and they too are moving forward – *onward and upward*.

And yes, I've found love again. I have an amazing man in my life who respects me, loves me and brings a sense of lightness and joy to every moment, from the mundane to the marvelous. Will this relationship last forever? I don't know. I hope so. But what I do know is that, for now, it's joyful, healthy and exactly what I need.

Is life perfect? No.

But do I believe that with resilience, determination and relentless optimism, life can and will be wonderful?

Absolutely and resoundingly yes.

And it can be for you too.

The Beginning

THE RELENTLESS OPTIMISM COMPANION WORKBOOKS & JOURNALS

Dive deeper into your journey of *Relentless Optimism* with a powerful collection of workbooks and journals crafted to help you live a more empowered, joyful and purpose-driven life. Each workbook aligns with the transformative principles of *Relentless Optimism & Other Life Goals*, offering practical tools to help you track progress, nurture gratitude and achieve your dreams.

Here's a sneak peek at what's ahead:

Relentless Gratitude: Journaling Your Way to Abundance

Embrace the power of gratitude with this guided journal designed to help you celebrate life's beautiful moments from the small to the momentous. Cultivate a daily practice of joy and abundance as you rediscover the magic in every day.

Relentless Self-Care: Prioritize, Thrive, Repeat

Make self-care a priority! This journal will help you create sustainable habits for rest, reflection and recharging – all rooted in optimism. Your well-being deserves dedicated space, and this journal helps you protect it.

Relentless Productivity: The Optimist's Lists of To-Dos

Stay organized and inspired with this uplifting productivity planner. With each list and reminder, tackle your daily tasks with purpose and positivity, bringing you one step closer to your goals.

Relentless Insight: Your Story, Journey, Dreams & Discoveries

Unleash your inner storyteller with this open-format journal, perfect for capturing dreams, reflections and insights. This is your space to express, explore and savor the art of writing without limits.

Relentless Focus: Tracking Goals with Purpose & Optimism

Bring your goals to life with this goal-tracking workbook! Whether you're aiming for short-term wins or lifelong achievements, this tool keeps you motivated, grounded and optimistic as you make progress toward your dreams.

Get Ready to Thrive!
These workbooks are designed to empower every step of your journey so you can embrace a life of relentless optimism and make your dreams a reality. Afterall, living the life you've imagined is absolutely attainable – all it takes is the work to get there.

Stay tuned for the official release!
Visit www.relentlessoptimism.org to learn more, and subscribe to the Relentless Optimism Newsletter for updates, tips, exclusive content … and, of course, a regular dose of positivity and motivation.

About the Author

Rya Hazelwood is an entrepreneur, corporate marketing executive, devoted mother of boys and avid traveler. She is also a survivor – overcoming emotional and narcissistic abuse, toxic relationships and the challenges of rebuilding her life as a single parent. Through every role and obstacle, Rya's relentless optimism has been her guiding force, propelling her toward healing, success and fulfillment both personally and professionally.

As an author and motivational speaker, Rya captivates audiences with her heartfelt storytelling, seamlessly blending honesty, humor and wisdom. Her work explores themes of personal empowerment, resilience and the courage to rise above life's darkest moments. By sharing her journey, she inspires others to break free from toxic cycles, trust their inner voices and boldly create lives filled with purpose, joy and authenticity.

Rya is a firm believer in the transformative power of mindset, championing the idea that even the smallest shifts in perspective can spark profound change. Her mission is to empower others to move forward – onward and upward – with courage, grace and relentless optimism.

Rya lives in Atlanta, Georgia, with her two sons, where she continues to write, speak and inspire.

For more, visit ryahazelwood.com or follow her on:
Instagram: instagram.com/relentless.optimism.xo
Facebook: facebook.com/Relentless.Optimism.XO
or TikTok: www.tiktok.com/@relentless.optimism

For additional resources to support you on your journey, visit ryahazelwood.com/additional-resources.

Relentless Optimism
IG@relentless.optimism.xo
www.relentlessoptimism.org

Made in the USA
Columbia, SC
07 February 2025